kids' crafternoon
felting

kids' crafternoon
felting

25 projects for a crafty afternoon

edited by Kathreen Ricketson

hardie grant books
MELBOURNE · LONDON

Contents

Introduction

Do you like to create something every day? Are you often doodling or daydreaming in class, constantly making up creations in your head, figuring out how you could make or invent something new? Or perhaps you love nothing better than to rummage in the craft box or fabric bin to get some inspiration. If this sounds like you, then this book will help you on your journey to create and make cool, unique stuff!

Get arty and crafty

Almost the best thing about making stuff is that you get to constantly learn new skills: figuring out instructions and working out how to get your materials to do what you want them to do uses both sides of your brain. So making stuff is not just about being artsy or craftsy, it's about problem solving, project planning, artistic endeavour, and even some maths and science sneak in there too! When you sit down to create something, whether it's your own original idea or something from a pattern, it involves a whole heap of learning processes, and has the bonus effect of invigorating your spirit. Seriously, making stuff is fun: part mess, part creation, part community and part experimentation. So next time you want to get creative, why not invite a friend over and have a crafternoon party?

A feeling for felt

The projects in this book are all about using and making felt. You will learn what felt is, how it's made and how to make it yourself, and how to use a whole stack of designs and patterns. You will be sewing and gluing and learning a few new skills along the way. You can make most of the designs in this book with just a little bit of felt and some basic tools, and most of the designs can be mixed up and mashed up to create your own interpretation – or you could take a little inspiration from within these pages to create your own designs from scratch! Whatever you decide, and whatever your crafting style, first read up on the techniques and materials section before you get started. Make sure you follow the safety advice when handling hot and sharp tools. So grab a snack plate, put on some inspirational music and get creative!

Tools and Materials

All the projects in this book use felt as their base. Felt is a non-woven cloth made with matted-together woollen fibres. There are lots of different kinds of felt materials, some are soft and light, others stiff and tough. Felt is used in all sorts of industrial, commercial and domestic situations, and has a long and ancient history. Today it is used to make hats, shoes, home furnishings, and textile art. And did you know that nomadic people in Central Asia still use felt to make their yurts (tents).

FELT

The felt you will be using in this book is broken into three main types:

- Felt craft sheets
- Wet felt
- Fulled recycled-jumper felt

Felt craft sheets are found in most craft shops, and come in a range of colours, thicknesses and quality.

- Acrylic felt and eco-felt are widely available in craft stores and are made from 100 per cent synthetic acrylic plastic. Eco-felt's difference is that it is made from recycled plastic bottles rather than brand-new plastic pellets. Acrylic felt comes in a huge range of colours and can be sewn and glued. It tends to be thin and itchy and not for projects that will be washed and worn. Plus it is flammable!

- Wool-blend felt can be found in most good sewing and craft shops. It is usually 30 per cent wool and 70 per cent rayon. Rayon is a semi-synthetic fibre, which means that while it comes from a natural source (wood pulp) it goes through quite a few manufacturing processes so that it can be used as a fibre. It is soft and strong, comes in lots of lovely colours and can be used for most craft and sewing applications.

- 100 per cent wool felt is a natural choice: it can be sewn, glued and needle felted. It is warm, soft and fire resistant. However, it can be a bit thicker than wool-blend felt and might be more difficult to work with on some finer projects. It is also more expensive, harder to find and doesn't come in the same range of bright colours as acrylic felt.

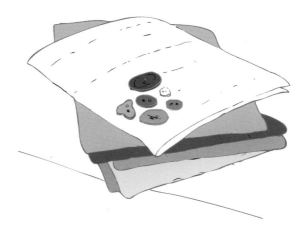

Wet felting. You can make your own felt sheets and shaped objects with wool roving (the brushed wool that comes direct from the sheep's back) and some warm soapy water. To make your own felt using the wet felting method, you need to create fine layers of roving going in a crisscross pattern. Dampen it all down with warm soapy water and then agitate it by rubbing, rolling and pressing the fibres together until they compact into a solid shape. You can make flat sheets or shape it into all sorts of different objects. The material that you end up with will depend upon how much roving you used and how much agitation you gave it. You can make very fine and delicate felt using this process or very sturdy thick felt – it's great to experiment with.

Fulling is the process of turning woollen fabric – either woven or knitted – into felt by agitating and shrinking it in hot soapy water (it's easiest to do this in the washing machine). You need 100 per cent woollen fabric for this process: knitted wool jumpers and scarves are perfect, but woollen woven fabric (think wool suits and skirts) can be made into felt too. The material that results from this process is vastly variable: it depends on the initial fabric and how long you wash and shrink it for.

Once you have fulled your woollen material, you will then need to deconstruct it. This is the process of cutting the garment up and salvaging all the usable bits. This felt material can be used for just about any of the projects in this book (except small toys and delicate sewn items that need fine materials).

WOOL SUPPLIES

Wool felt sheets. These are a bit more luxurious and expensive than acrylic craft felt. You can buy them from good craft, wool and sewing shops.

Wool roving is a bundle of wool fibres, from a sheep's fleece, that have been washed, combed and prepared ready for spinning into wool yarn. Wool roving can be purchased in small amounts that have already been dyed into lots of different colours. You can find these readily at craft and wool shops.

Wool yarn. This is wool that has been spun into yarn: it is used for knitting, crochet and stitching and comes in a huge range of thicknesses and colours. You can pick up a ball of wool yarn at any craft or wool shop.

Felt balls. These are small balls of felted wool fibres. They come in various sizes from 1 cm up to 10 cm and are available in a huge range of colours too. They are made with wool roving which you wrap up in a ball, wet with warm soapy water and roll in your hands for a few minutes until it turns into felt. They are quick and fun to make and you will be making some for the projects in this book. You can also find them in good craft supply stores and sometimes bead and wool shops.

OTHER SUPPLIES

Toy filling. You will need to have some stuffing on hand to fill your stuffed toys when you make them. You can purchase toy filling from craft stores or you can recycle old pillows and use their stuffing again.

Threads. You will need some regular cotton or polyester sewing machine thread for your sewing machine. Don't buy the super-cheap stuff as it can break easily and wreck your machine. You will also need some embroidery threads, sometimes called embroidery floss: these are heavier cotton threads that are used with a hand-sewing needle to decorate and embellish.

Glue

- Hot glue gun and glue sticks. Nothing quite beats the instant satisfaction or the permanent fixing ability of a glue gun. While a glue gun is a useful craft tool, it can cause burns so careful use is essential. As a general rule, a small amount goes a long way and you must avoid your hands coming into direct contact with the glue. Also remember when using a glue gun to put some pressure on the top surface for a few seconds after you have applied the glue, as this helps to make the pieces stick together.
- PVA craft glue is a non-toxic multi-purpose glue. It can be used on all sorts of surfaces, including wood, paper, fabric, felt and beads. It goes on white but then dries clear.

- Regular school glue stick is usually water soluble and non-toxic. As well as for paper projects, glue sticks are great to use in place of pins to hold fabric in place while you sew.

Craft essentials. Rickrack, ribbons, feathers, buttons, wire, craft magnets, pipe cleaners, Velcro, craft glue, press studs, safety pins, elastic hair bands, and elastic: these are all pretty self explanatory and can be found at craft stores or even your local shops.

Jewellery findings. Ring blanks, brooch backs, beads, chain, cord and clear elastic cord can all be found at craft, sewing or bead shops.

Embellishments. You can jazz up your projects with collected fun bits such as beads, embroidery thread, mini pompoms, fancy trim, ribbon, and buttons. Keep a box with your collection of bits and pieces to use when you need them.

PROTECTIVE MATERIALS

When painting, gluing or doing any messy work, first spread out *newspaper* to protect your work surface.

A plastic apron, old work shirt or other *protective clothing* is useful to have on hand when doing any messy work too.

TOOLS

You don't need many tools for the projects in this book. A sewing machine is great; however, if you don't have access to one, all of the sewn projects can be hand sewn. You will also need a basic hand-sewing kit, scissors, ruler and thread and you are set to go.

Hand-sewing kit

You can purchase a sewing kit already made up at a craft or sewing store, or you can make up your own: keep all your sewing supplies in a small plastic container, a sewing basket or even a clear glass jar. Make the 'Designer wallet' on page 72 — it would make an excellent holder for a little sewing kit. Fill your sewing kit with these supplies:

- Small snipping scissors
- Pins and a small pincushion (sew some elastic around your pincushion to create a wrist pin cushion)
- Hand-sewing needles in a couple of sizes: smaller needles for regular thread and larger embroidery needles for decorative stitching.

- Sewing thread and embroidery thread (or embroidery floss) in several basic colours
- Seam ripper (unpicker) is essential
- Thimble
- Pencil

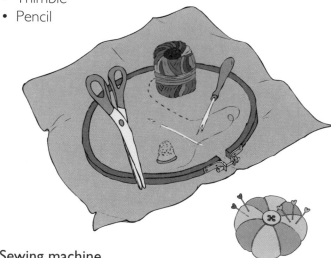

Sewing machine

- You will need a sewing machine for some of the projects in this book: it doesn't have to be fancy — a simple second-hand sewing machine will do — as long as it can do straight stitch and maybe zigzag, you are set.
- It is important to care for your machine. Take it for a regular service and learn how to clean it properly. Use the small tool kit (and manual) that comes with your machine (usually a small screwdriver, lint brush, sewing machine oil, and tweezers) to maintain it and learn how to thread it correctly.
- Your sewing machine will come with a presser foot and a throat plate with markings on it: use these to guide your seam allowance when sewing, and to help you to keep a straight seam. The bobbin is the small spool of thread underneath the throat plate; you will need to refill this when it runs out.

- Fill a few bobbins with the thread that you are using, so you don't have to stop and start in the middle of a project.
- Check that you have a good desk light and that your seat is comfortable: you don't want to strain your eyes or back!
- Make sure you have a spare sewing machine needle or two. It's very annoying to have your last needle break when you are in the middle of a project. You will use universal sewing machine needles in the projects in this book.
- Check your stitch tension by doing a sewing test on a bit of scrap fabric. The upper and lower tensions must be balanced to produce a perfect stitch on both sides. Refer to the sewing machine manual if you need to change the tension.
- Keep your pins and pincushion near your sewing machine. A small pair of scissors to snip threads and a seam ripper (unpicker) are also good to have on hand.

- Thread your sewing machine with a neutral-coloured thread, such as grey or cream, or use the same colour as your fabric. Fill your bobbin with the same colour thread.
- Set your sewing machine to a straight stitch and use a medium length (2.5) stitch, unless otherwise specified in your project instructions.

BASIC EQUIPMENT

Iron. You will use an iron to press seams as you sew and to press your final project. Remember to press, not glide, to prevent any stretching of fabric. Use an ironing board or lay out a towel onto your table.

Scissors. You will need three basic types of scissors: small, sharp scissors for clipping seams and snipping threads; a really good pair of fabric scissors that you should use for fabric only (using them on paper will dull the blades); and a pair of general scissors, for everything else.

OTHER USEFUL TOOLS

Tape measure and ruler. You will need a good, wide ruler and a tape measure. The ruler is handy for drawing and cutting straight lines and the tape measure is good for measuring around curves, things and people.

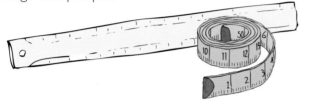

Use *tracing paper* or plain brown craft paper to trace your templates.

Use a *chopstick or pencil* to help turn small sewn objects right side out and to push stuffing into corners and tight spots when making soft toys.

Awl and bone folder. These are bookbinding and card-making tools and can be found in a general craft store. A scoring knife or bone folder is used to score paper (scoring creates a line or depression in heavier card that will help you create an even crease when you fold). You can substitute a butter knife, and you will also need a ruler. An awl is basically a sharp, heavy needle with a handle on the end, that is used to punch fine holes into thick paper, card or through many layers of paper at once. You can substitute a heavy darning needle or small craft hole punch (or even a nail).

NEEDLE-FELTING SUPPLIES

Needle felting (also called dry felting) is the process of meshing wool fibres with a needle. A special long, sharp needle is used to repeatedly stab into the wool roving: the needle catches and tangles the wool fibre and it begins to tighten. Needle felting can be used to make small wool sculptures; however, in this book it is only used to decorate and embellish. You will need:

Long felting needles. These are not like sewing needles, they have a curve or a handle at the top to help you hold the needle in your hand, and the needle is triangular rather than round in shape, with barbs sticking out at the pointed tip. These needles are strong and extremely sharp. The barbs on the tip are essential to catch and tangle and felt the wool fibres, so you need to be very careful when using these special tools. Felting needles really hurt if you accidentally stab yourself, so work slowly and carefully and keep your hands well clear.

Dense foam pad is required to protect your work surface and your project and to stop your needle breaking. Use high-quality foam from a craft or hardware store.

Basic Techniques

HOW TO FELT A WOOL JUMPER

Don't throw out your pure wool jumpers: you can felt them in your washing machine and then use them to make all sorts of things. This felting process (called fulling) takes knitted (or woven) woollen fabric and mats the fibres together so you can cut the piece without the stitches unravelling. All you need to do is wash the jumper in the washing machine on a long, hot setting with a little detergent to soften the fibres. For the fulling to work the jumper needs to be made of 100 per cent wool and not treated to be machine washable.

1. Start with a 100 per cent wool jumper – you can often find these at second-hand clothing stores or charity shops. You will need to read the labels when looking for second-hand jumpers (make sure they really are wool) and choose light- to medium-weight ones: the really heavy thick ones will felt up too thick to sew through easily.
2. Throw your wool jumpers into the washing machine, set it on the heavy duty setting with hot water, add a small amount of dishwashing detergent (a short squirt will do). You can do this process by hand in the kitchen sink but it's hard work and takes quite a bit of muscle and energy.
3. When the wash cycle is done, check to see if the jumper is felted to your liking – the wool knit should have thickened, and will be fuzzier and shrunken in size. It can take one to three washings to properly felt a wool jumper – try washing jeans at the same time to give extra agitation and friction in the water. Check the jumper after each washing since jumpers can felt at differing rates and, once they felt, they can continue to felt further and shrink in size with each subsequent washing. You can either air dry or dry the felted jumpers in the dryer.

TAKING APART A FELTED JUMPER

Many of the projects in this book will require you to deconstruct your jumper once it is felted. What this means is for you to save the good bits and ditch the rest. However, there are a couple of projects where you will start with an intact felted jumper so make sure you check the project instructions before chopping the jumper up.

1. Cut along the side seams, as close to the seam as possible on each side – you will throw out the bulky seam bit. Then cut off the arms in the same way, close to each side of the seams. You could use the arms for the 'Upcycled wristies' on page 26 or you could cut the seam open and use the felt fabric in another project.

2. Don't discard interesting pockets and seams as these can often be used for creative effects in your projects. You will want to snip off the buttons and save these and possibly snip off the neck ribbing too.

WET FELTING

Wet felting is clean messy fun. It involves water, soap and wool and lots of rolling, pressing and hitting! You will be using hot water and soap to mesh together the wool fibres, and then you will massage and mangle the felt until it turns into a dense matted textile. You can get lots of different textures, weights and shapes of felt using this process – it's fun to experiment. Wet felting involves a couple of stages, but neither of them difficult.

Stage one is to lay out your fibres in several crisscross layers, then dampen them, press and roll gently until the fibres bond.

Stage two is where things get rough! Once the fibres are bonded, you can hit, slap, bang and roll your piece until it shrinks and becomes strong and dense.

What you need:
• Wool roving in different colours
• Bubble wrap
• Hot water
• A few drops of liquid dishwashing detergent
• Old towels

How to do it:

1. Lay a towel or mat down onto your table to catch the water, then lay a piece of bubble wrap on top. The bubble wrap needs to be as big as your project.

2. Pull and tease out thin strands of wool roving and lay it out in a fine layer with all the fibres lying in the same direction on top of the bubble wrap. Then add a second layer of fibres, this time with them all lying across the first layer of fibres. Repeat this process so you have four layers of fibres. Check the layers to see that there are no thin spots. Lastly, lay some contrasting coloured wool roving in a decorative design on top, in any direction you like.

3. Pour a little hot, soapy water over the felt (this is why you laid the towel down first), and gently press it with your hands as you slowly pour the water over it, being careful not to move the layers or mess up your design. Then lay another sheet of bubble wrap over the top. Roll up your layers carefully.

4. Firmly but carefully massage and roll the felt. You will need to roll it between 50 and 100 times to get a firm felt material. Don't press too hard at first; gradually add pressure as you go. Every 20–30 rolls, unroll and check it by gently pulling at it with your fingers to see if it is strongly bonded. If it pulls apart, add more hot water and carry on with the process for a while longer. Once it is all densely matted up, rinse the soap out in cold water.

5. Now comes the fulling stage, where you turn your matted fibre sheet into a strong, tough felt. Get mad at it: throw it, crunch it up, hit and bang it with a rolling pin or meat tenderiser, and roll and press and squeeze it until it has shrunk some more and is really tough and strong. You can do this stage for a short time to create a delicate material or for a

long time if you want your felt fabric to be thicker – it's up to you: experiment!

6. To finish, lay the felt out on a dry towel, pull and stretch at the edges to smooth and even it out, roll it in up in the dry towel and squeeze as much water out as you can. You can leave it to dry flat on a towel, or if you want a really smooth finish you can press it with a warm steam iron first then leave it to finish drying.

MAKING FELT BALLS

This is the same principal as wet felting, only you are using a small amount of felt and rolling it in the palm of your hand. You can use this technique to make balls, cubes, fake rocks, and even love hearts!

Take a piece of wool roving and roll it up into a neat ball, dip it in warm soapy water and begin by gently massaging it in the palm of your hand in a circular motion. Dunk the ball in more warm soapy water and keep on rolling in the palm of your hand. You will feel it get firmer and firmer, if you want a tight small ball, you can roll it really hard to compress it, or if you want a light ball you can continue rolling it gently. Press it in a towel and leave to dry (if you make enough, put them in a stocking and pop them in the dryer if you like).

Experiment with size and shape, you can make bigger balls and tiny, wee balls – depending upon how much wool roving you start out with and how firmly you roll the ball in your hands.

NEEDLE FELTING

You will find an introduction to needle felting in the 'Upcycled wristies' project on page 26 where needle felting is used as an interesting way to add detail and decoration to a project. Basically what you are doing is fusing another layer of fibre onto your base felted fabric. Needle felting takes patience and care. It takes a while for the wool roving to begin to bond properly at first – you need to have patience and just keep poking your needle in and out until you notice the fleece begin to shrink around where you are needling.

You will need a special barb-tipped felting needle and some dense foam matting to do this. You can find these at any craft store. You will also need wool roving and the project that you are embellishing must also be made of 100 per cent wool.

How to do it:

1. Place the wool fabric that you are embellishing onto your foam mat, then lay the wool roving onto the fabric in your desired design. Try some simple geometric shapes at first, but once you get good at it you can be more adventurous.

2. Take your barbed needle and begin to poke the needle (up and down, not at an angle) into your wool roving (keeping your hands out of the way). Random is fine: you don't need to rush or poke it hard, just poke it in about 1cm each time through the wool roving and into the wool sheet. Be careful where your fingers are – the needle is very sharp!

3. Continue poking the needle up and down until the fibres have compressed and you can see the outline of your shape. Keep going until the wool roving is really compacted into the wool sheet and cannot come out when you pull at it with your fingers.

4. Pull it off the foam mat – it might have become a bit stuck, but just carefully remove it – and if some of the wool fibres come loose, just work them back in with the needle.

SEWING

Hand stitches

Running stitch. This is the simplest and most commonly used hand stitch. Pass the needle in and out of the fabric, keeping the length and the space of the stitches the same each time.

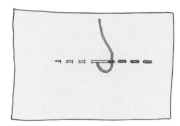

Whipstitch. This is a very basic over-and-over stitch that is used for joining fabric pieces. Insert the needle into the fabric at the same angle each time.

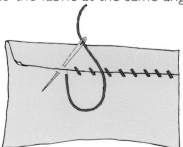

Backstitch. This stitch is very useful for drawing with thread. Take a backward stitch then bring the needle through in front of the first stitch.

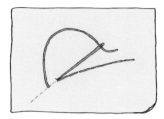

Blanket stitch. This stitch is used to reinforce edges. Working from left to right, insert the needle in the upper line and stitch straight down, keeping the thread under the point of the needle. Pull up the stitch to form a loop, and repeat.

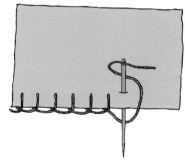

Cross stitch. This is probably the most widely used embroidery stitch; it forms a simple cross shape. Place your first stitch on a diagonal and then the second stitch is crossed over the top in the opposite direction.

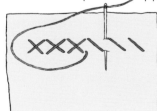

French knot. This is a decorative stitch made by looping the thread several times around the needle before inserting it into the fabric. It is used to create fine details such as animal eyes and the centre of a flower. Start from the back of your fabric and bring your needle through to the front. Pull the thread all the way through and then wrap it around your needle a couple of times then, holding the thread tight, push your needle back down into the fabric, just a millimetre or so away from where you brought the needle up. It is important to push the needle slowly through to the other side while holding the knot in place with your other hand or thumb.

Basic sewing tips

- When you pin the fabric pieces together, make sure that the good sides are facing each other, and that the seams are on the 'wrong' side. When using felt this is less important as there are usually no wrong or right sides with felt.
- When pinning, place the pins at right angles to the fabric edge with the pin head facing outwards: this makes it much easier to remove the pins while you are sewing on a machine. Remove pins as you come to them, as sewing over a pin could break your needle. Some of the projects in this book suggest using a glue stick to hold your felt pieces together while sewing: this can be an excellent, less fiddly, alternative to pins.
- The seam allowance is the amount of space between the stitching line and the edge of the fabric: try to keep this to about 1 cm, and use the edge of the sewing machine's foot or the lines on the throat plate of your machine as a guide to help you keep your seams straight.
- When sewing a straight line be sure to backstitch at the beginning and end to ensure your stitches don't unravel.

Sewing a button

Adding buttons to your projects is a really cute way of embellishing them as well as being practical sometimes too. If you want to get fancy with your buttons you could choose two buttons that fit on top of each other and sew them at the same time.

1. First mark with pencil where the buttons will go. Thread a small needle with about 60 cm of sewing thread, double it over so you have about 30 cm of doubled thread, and knot the end.
2. Pull the needle through from the back of your material at the marked spot and up through one hole of the button. Put your needle back in through the other hole of the button and back through your material at the marked point. Pull the thread firmly. Repeat this three times through each buttonhole.
3. Finish by pushing the needle and thread through to the back of the material. Before pulling the thread tight, thread your needle through the loop of thread then pull tight to form a knot.

SAFETY

Sewing machines

- A sewing machine has a sharp needle that goes up and down very quickly, so it is important to keep your fingers away from the needle while it is moving.
- Use controlled movements while the machine is running and avoid placing your fingers in front of the needle; instead, guide your object from the side of the needle's path.
- Don't look away from the machine while it is running.
- Gather all your materials, tools and supplies before you start to sew. Trace and cut out your pattern pieces, set up your sewing machine, check the lighting and your chair for comfort.

Irons

An iron can cause burn injuries if you are not careful. Be sure to keep your iron away from younger people and keep the cord away from tripping feet.

- Iron on a high, stable surface such as an ironing board or table. Don't use the iron on the floor.
- Unplug the iron immediately after use, and remember that the iron can take a while to cool down after it is turned off.

Scissors

Scissors have sharp tips and blades. Be sure to put them away when you have finished with them.

- Don't walk around carrying scissors or wave them around while talking.
- Watch where you are cutting, and keep your fingers out of the way.
- Store your scissors in a safe place out of reach of younger people.

Awls

- Don't leave your awl around for smaller people to play with, and always replace it in its safety sleeve when you are finished with it.
- Watch where you poke it. Be careful to protect your workbench and your hands when you are using it.

Hot glue guns

- Choose a craft glue gun rather than a carpenter's glue gun, as a craft glue gun has a lower temperature and therefore is not as dangerous. (It is still hot enough to burn you!)
- Be sure to use the correct glue sticks for your glue gun.
- Wear protective clothing and protect your work surface. Be careful to hold the glue gun over the table surface so as not to drip the hot glue onto your skin or clothing. Use it only on the table, never leave it on the floor and keep the electrical cord out of reach and away from tripping feet.
- Don't forget to turn the glue gun off when it is not in use.

pep your look

Making your own accessories *means you can show your individual style.*
No one else will have that exact hat made from recycled clothing, or be
wearing a ring like the one you hand sewed from woollen felt. You will not only
have a unique look, but will also be expressing your own personal style:
a career in fashion could be your next step!

The projects in this section are fairly easy and fun to make. You will learn a
couple of ways to make your own felt and some basic hand-sewing techniques too.
It doesn't matter if you are a boy or a girl, there is a project here for you.
And just remember that you don't have to make it exactly as shown in the picture:
feel free to add your own personal touch to make it truly yours. So get ready to create!
You will need music, snacks, a clear space and a comfy chair.
Gather up your materials and get felting.

Stitched Jewels

Make a pendant and ring by playing with colours and shapes! Mix and match until you find a look you love, then sew it all together with some creative stitches. You will use a little bit of hand stitching for this project and will need a few tiny scraps of felt and some colourful buttons from your collection.

project by: cassi griffin
suitable for: beginners
should take: less than an hour

SHOPPING LIST

- 1.5 cm button for each ring and pendant
- Scraps of colourful wool or craft felt
- Embroidery thread or floss
- Crochet or knitting yarn, string, hemp, leather or chain for a pendant
- Ring finding with a flat top

CRAFTY NEEDS

- Scissors
- Embroidery needle
- Fabric glue for pendant
- Hot glue gun for ring

GET READY

- Gather your tools and materials and clear some space on a sturdy work table. Make sure you have a comfy chair and some good lighting.
- Take care when using a hot glue gun and scissors. Read the section on page 19 about safe handling of these tools and be sure to put everything away when you are done.
- You'll be doing some hand-sewing, but don't worry if you have never sewn before. Your stitches don't have to be perfect, and you will find some sewing basics on page 17, but you will need a basic sewing kit (page 11) to get started.

HOW TO MAKE

1. Cut out the shapes

Choose three colours of felt from your felt scraps. From each colour cut three circles for your ring and three squares for your pendant. The smallest shape should be 1.5 cm wide and each other shape 5 mm larger on all sides. Start with the smallest shape – either a square or a circle – and cut around your button, leaving a 5 mm border for decorative stitching.

2. Make layers

Place your shape on top of the next colour and trim around it leaving a 5 mm border for your stitching. Repeat for the third layer.

3. Stack 'em up

Stack your shapes with the button on top. Sew the button through all three layers, using three strands of embroidery thread or floss. Choose another three strands of contrasting floss and sew decorative stitches on each felt layer. Simple running stitch will be enough, but if you want to try small blanket stitches or cross stitches on the edging, that would be very pretty too.

4. For the ring

Place a dab of glue from your hot glue gun to attach the decorated, layered circle to the flat area of the ring finding. Take care with hot glue: the hot glue will also make the metal ring hot.

5. For the pendant

Cut another square slightly smaller than the largest layer of your pendant. Place a line of fabric glue along the top and bottom of your square and glue it to the back of your pendant. Measure a length of yarn or chain so that your pendant will easily fit over your head. When the glue has dried, thread the length of yarn or chain through the square and tie the ends together to finish your necklace.

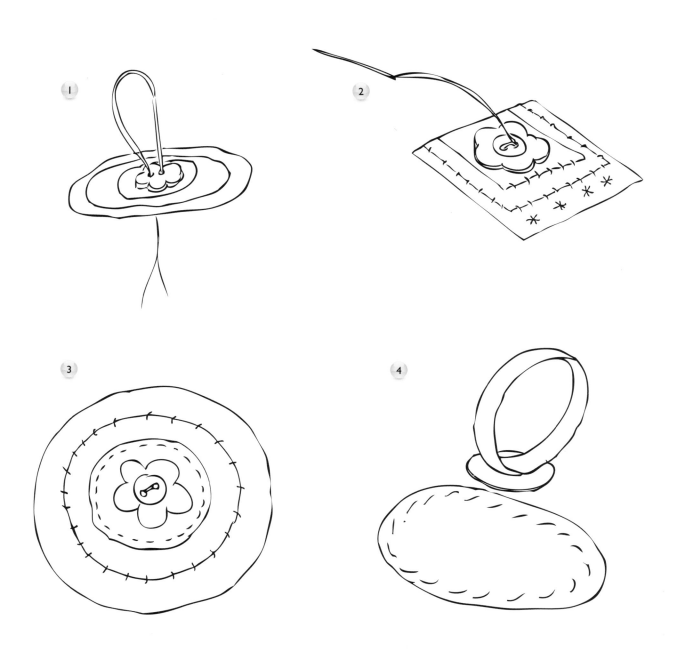

Upcycled Wristies

These super easy-to-make wrist warmers will keep your hands toasty warm and looking great. The mitts are made from felted recycled jumpers from a second-hand store. Choose jumpers that are 100 per cent wool and of medium size. In this project you will learn how to add your own unique design using the needle felting technique.

project by: suzie fry
suitable for: beginners
should take: less than an hour

SHOPPING LIST

- Second-hand wool jumper suitable for felting
- Wool roving in a few colours
- Cotton thread for sewing

CRAFTY NEEDS

- Ruler
- Scissors (fabric scissors and small snipping scissors)
- Pins
- Hand-sewing kit or a sewing machine
- Foam mat and needle-felting needle

GET READY

- Gather your tools and materials and clear some space on a sturdy work table. Because you are working with felt fibres you need to make sure to have a clean space to work on. Make sure you have a comfy chair and some good lighting.
- Take care when using an iron, scissors or felting needle. Read the section on page 19 about safety and put everything away carefully when you are done.
- This project requires some simple sewing, but don't worry if you have never sewn before. Your stitches don't have to be perfect. If you are using a sewing machine, read up on the basics on page 11 and, if you plan on hand-sewing, you will need a basic sewing kit (page 11) to get started.
- Here you will be making your own felt with recycled woollen clothing and you will also be learning how to do some basic needle felting. See pages 16–17 for more information on these processes.

HOW TO MAKE

1. Felt your woollen jumpers

Start by felting your jumper (see the instructions on page 14 for this process). If you are making your mitts from the sleeves of a jumper, use an adult size jumper, otherwise any jumper will be fine.

2. Make your mitts

If modifying the sleeves of a felted jumper, start by cutting the sleeves off the jumper and then put your arms into the sleeves to make sure they fit. To make the sewn version of these mitts you will be using the body of the felted jumper (see diagram 1). First measure around your forearm and hand to work out the width, then measure up your arm from the centre of your middle finger to midway along your forearm (or the wrist) to find the length. These ones measure 20 cm long and the fabric was 15 cm wide at the top and 17 cm wide at the bottom. Draw this shape onto a piece of paper to create a pattern.

3. For the sewn version

Using the body of the felted jumper, cut it up as per the diagram below. This will make two flat pieces. Then lay out one of the pieces and place your paper pattern on top of it with the cuff end lying against the hem of the jumper. Keep your pattern piece in line with the knitting, running up and down its length, so that your felt has more stretch in it from side to side than from top to bottom. Repeat the process to make your second mitt.

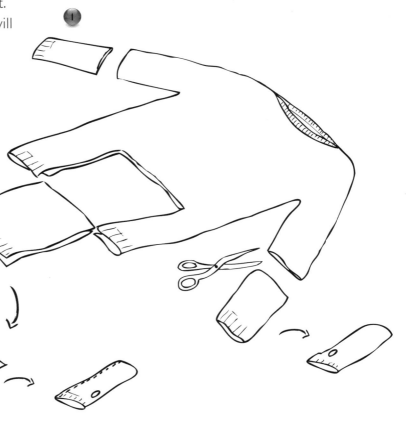

4. Cut a thumbhole

Measure 5 cm from the hem side of your fabric piece and place a mark in the centre point of your fabric. Cut a small hole, with your small pointy scissors, about as big as a five-cent piece. Poke your thumb in to check the size: if it is uncomfortably tight, keep adjusting it a tiny bit at a time until it fits your thumb snugly (remember it will stretch a bit as you wear the mitts). When you cut your second thumbhole, remember to make it a mirror image of the first.

5. Needle felt your mitts

Needle felting is used here to decorate the mitts, but you could stitch or appliqué your chosen design if you like. Slide the foam mat inside your sleeve or underneath your felt fabric. Place wool roving in a pleasing design over your felt fabric (see diagram 2). To felt the roving into your wool felt base permanently, you need to repeatedly push the needle in and out over and over all along your roving design. Each needle puncture makes a little knot inside the felt that ties the two layers together and at the same time shrinks the roving down into the felt. The more needle pushes, the stronger the bond will be. If you don't needle enough times or evenly all over, fibres will work loose over time and come away. The more design elements you add, the thicker and sturdier your mitts will be.

Make a mirror image of your design on the other mitt if you want matching mitts, or make a different design if you like. When you have finished needling your design, carefully pull the mitt away from the foam. Some of the fleece fibres will be visible on the underside: this is fine.

6. Finishing the mitts

If you used the sleeve of a jumper you are finished at this point: there is no sewing to do. If you started with flat pieces you need to sew them together into a tube shape either by hand or by machine. Fold your flat piece with the long edges together, pin and sew with the right sides on the outside. To finish, sew a straight seam all the way along this long edge. Remember that this seam will be visible and forms a part of your design, so keep your sewing as a straight as possible.

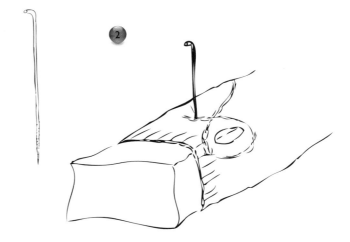

Sweet Felt Acorns

There are so many crafty possibilities when you have acorn caps and wool roving. In this project you will first learn to wet felt a scented ball. Wet felting is when you take wool roving, warm soapy water, and use a lot of agitation to bind the wool fibres together to create a hard shape. Then you could create a pendant for a necklace, or make a bowl of scented, felt-filled acorns.

project by: laura malek
suitable for: beginners
should take: 1–2 hours

SHOPPING LIST

- Wool roving in different colours
- Acorn caps
- 5 mm wide ribbon, 25 cm per acorn
- Rope cord or chain for necklace

CRAFTY NEEDS

- Large bowl
- Small bowl
- Very warm water (4 cups)
- Cold water (¾ cup)
- Essential oil – rose, lavender or orange works really well
- Awl
- Liquid dishwashing detergent
- Towel
- Baking pan

- Scissors
- Craft glue
- Spoon
- Smock to keep you dry
- Embroidery needle

GET READY

- Gather your tools and materials and clear some space on a sturdy work table. Because you are working with felt fibres you need to make sure to have a clean space to work on. Make sure you have a comfy chair and some good lighting.
- Take care when using sharp needles. Read the section on page 19 about safety and be sure to put everything away carefully when you are done.
- This project requires making felt balls from wool roving, but don't worry if you have never done this before. It's fun and messy, and you can read about making your own felt on page 16. Wool roving is sold in most craft stores and comes in many colours.

HOW TO MAKE

1. Prepare your acorn cap

Choose your acorn wisely; a hard, sturdy cap works best for the pendant. Prep your acorn caps by poking a hole through the top for the ribbon. Using two fingers, hold the acorn cap open face down on an old towel. Take the awl (or a nail) in your other hand and press firmly into the centre of the acorn, or off-centre if there is a stem (see diagram 1). Make sure not to punch it, as this will crack the acorn cap. The hole must be large enough for your needle and ribbon to go through.

2. Make the wet felt scented balls

This project should be done in the kitchen or, even better, outside, as it gets a little messy with the water and suds. Make sure you keep the strips of wool roving separate from the water area so they don't get wet before you need them to. Use the towel for both wiping up spills and drying your hands between each ball you make to keep the wool roving dry.

- Fill the large bowl with 4 cups of very warm water and 2 tablespoons of the liquid detergent. Stir quickly to create suds.
- Fill the small bowl with ¾ cup of cold water and 10–15 drops of the essential oil, and stir.
- Tear off a 5 cm x 2 cm piece of wool roving and roll it into a small tight ball. Holding onto the ball, place a very thin layer of roving around the ball.

With the ball tightly in your fingers, dip it into the bowl of warm soapy water. Pull out and start pinching and turning the ball between the first three fingers of both hands. Keep doing this until the ball cools off, and dip again. Continue to pinch and form the ball until it is firm (about 3 minutes). Once you have a firm, felted ball, place it into the bowl of cold water and essential oil. Let it sit for an hour, stirring every 10 minutes. Continue making more balls during this time.

- After an hour, spoon out the balls and place them on a plate to dry, after gently squeezing out some of the water. The drying process may take up to one day, so you may like to place them on a rack in the sun to dry or in a stocking in the tumble dryer.

3. Attach a string

If you are going to hang your acorns you should attach the string before gluing the felt ball in place. Cut off 25 cm of ribbon and thread it through your needle. Take your acorn cap and poke the needle through the underside of the acorn cap to the top. Turn your needle around and go through again, this time from the top of the acorn to the underside (see diagram 2). Release the ribbon. Both loose ends of the ribbon should be on the underside of the acorn cap, with a loop at the top. Tie a double knot to hold the loop in place.

4. Attach the acorn cap

Take your acorn cap and squirt a pea-size amount of glue into the middle of the underside (see diagram 3). Place a dry felted ball into the glue and hold it in place for 30 seconds until set. Set the felted acorn aside to dry for 10 minutes.

5. Acorn uses

Several of these scented balls in a bowl make wonderful air or drawer fresheners. If you want to use this as a necklace, attach a chain or cord onto the ribbon, long enough to hang around your neck. Or, if you want to use this as a window ornament, you could thread a longer string through the hole so that it can hang from a hook in the ceiling.

Upcycled Sherpa Hat

This warm and cosy ski-style Sherpa hat is made from recycled felted jumpers, and it includes optional pockets and tassels. Feel free to mix up your design any way you like; try different colour combinations or add some appliqué ideas from other projects in this book.

project by: lisa siebert
suitable for: confident beginners
should take: 1–2 hours

SHOPPING LIST

- Felted wool jumper (see page 14 for the felting process, making sure that the waistband and a side seam are usable)
- Contrasting coloured felted wool jumper for the earflaps and pocket
- 6 m chunky wool yarn in any colour
- Decorative button

CRAFTY NEEDS

- Sewing machine
- Iron
- Scissors
- Ruler
- Marking pen
- Pins
- Needle and thread
- Embroidery thread or floss
- Cutting mat

TEMPLATES

You will need the 'Sherpa hat' template for this project.

GET READY

- Gather your tools and materials and clear some space on a sturdy work table.
- Read the section on page 19 about safe handling of scissors and sharp needles.
- Trace or photocopy the templates onto paper. Cut them out and label them, then store them in an envelope so you can use them again and so they don't get wrecked.
- If using a sewing machine, read up on the basics on pages 11–12. If you plan on hand-sewing, you will need a basic sewing kit (page 11) to get started.
- You will make your felt from recycled woollen clothing – see page 14 for instructions

HOW TO MAKE

1. Cut out your main pieces

Trace the pattern and make three copies of each of the pieces. Lay out your jumper with the right side facing up and with double thickness, checking that the waistband is neatly aligned in both layers. Lay out the hat pattern on top of the felted jumper, with the bottom edge of the pattern against the ribbed edge of the jumper, and the left corner of the pattern touching the left seam of your sweater. Pin through all layers and trace around the pattern onto the jumper (see diagram 1).

2. Cut out contrasting pieces

Place your earflap pattern pieces on your contrasting sweater (again, on a double thickness of jumper). Trace, pin and cut out – you should end up with four pieces. Place your pocket pattern on an edge of this sweater; trace, pin and cut out.

3. Add decoration

Use a needle and embroidery thread or floss to sew a decorative button onto your pocket. Then place the pocket onto the hat piece and pin in place. You can choose where to place your pocket: it could be in the centre front, at the back or on one side. With your sewing machine and a simple straight stitch, sew your pocket onto your hat, sewing all the way around the 'curved' edge of the pocket but leaving the top 'straight' edge open. Set aside.

4. Make the ties

Cut 12 pieces of chunky wool yarn each 30 cm long, dividing them into four piles of three pieces each. Take two piles and tie a knot in the end of each of these sets, braid them together and stop 10 cm before you get to the end. Tie a knot here.

5. Make the tassels

Take the two remaining piles and cut them in half again. Take one pile of tassel lengths, set one length aside and place the other five lengths on top of the remaining yarn at the end of your braid, right next to the knot at the bottom of the tie. Lift one of the strands so that it sandwiches the tassel lengths in between the strands (see diagram 2). Grab the bottom two strands and the top strand and tie a tight knot right in the centre of the tassel lengths to secure them onto the tie. Take the remaining short length of yarn and tie a double knot about 1 cm down from where the tassel starts. Repeat for the other tassel. Trim and tuck in any yarn sticking out from your tassels.

6. Earflaps

Take your earflap pieces and lay the two backs on the table, with right sides facing up. Lay a braided tie down the centre of each with the top knot slightly below the bottom of the earflaps (check they are both the same length). Pin them in place with the knot centred at the bottom outer edge of the earflap. Place your other earflap piece on top, pin in place, then machine sew with a straight stitch around the curved edge leaving the top open (see diagram 3). Turn your earflaps right side out and lightly press the earflaps with a steam-iron on a 'wool' setting.

7. Assembling the hat

Pin the top edge of the earflap to the underside of the bottom edge of the hat, leaving a 1 cm overlap. Centre and align your earflaps with your hat. Flip your hat over so that the underside is facing up, and machine stitch the earflaps to the hat using a zigzag stitch. Then sew another row of zigzag stitches right next to the first row, to reinforce and tidy the raw edges.

With the wrong side of the hat facing out, gather the two outer corners of the bottom edge of the hat. Align the corners and pin them together. Sew all the way to the top of the hat, and then repeat on the other side. At the top of the hat gather the sections to form a cross and pin (see diagram 4), then sew them together. To finish, turn your hat right side out and press your seams with a steam iron on a 'wool' setting.

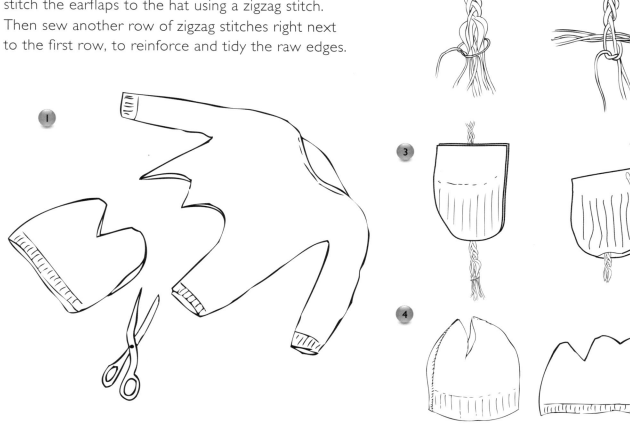

The Fascinator

Somewhere between a hat and a headband, this fascinator ticks all the boxes for cute and cool in one. Take some time to think about what colours you would like to wear: here we used grey with a pop of outrageous pink. You'll learn how to make a simple fabric flower and combine it with some felt leaves and feathers for seriously rocking headgear.

project by: nanette louchart-fletcher
suitable for: beginners
should take: 1–2 hours

SHOPPING LIST

- Headband
- Small selection of feathers
- Linen thread
- 10 cm square of felt
- 25 cm co-ordinating fabric
- Decorative button

CRAFTY NEEDS

- Hot glue gun
- Needle
- Scissors
- Hand-sewing kit

GET READY

- Gather your tools and materials and clear some space on a sturdy work table. Make sure you have a comfy chair and some good lighting.
- Take care when using a hot glue gun and scissors. Read the section on page 19 about safe handling of these items and be sure to put everything away carefully when you are done.
- You'll be doing some hand sewing, but don't worry if you have never sewn before. Your stitches don't have to be perfect, and you will find some sewing basics on page 17, but you will need a basic sewing kit (page 11) to get started.
- For this project you will be using wool felt or craft felt sheets. They are not expensive and are available in most craft or fabric shops. You will also need feathers (you can get these at a fishing or craft store).

HOW TO MAKE

1. Making the flower

Cut a 10 cm x 35 cm strip of fabric and a 30 cm piece of linen thread. Thread your needle and tie a secure knot in one end of the thread. Sew a running stitch along an imaginary centre line, running the length of the 35 cm strip (see diagram 1). Now slowly pull the thread until the fabric begins to bunch together. Continue to do this until the fabric has gathered together closely.

2. Finishing the flower

Turn your fabric over so that the wrong side is facing you and tightly roll the gathered fabric, starting where you began your running stitch. Wrap the tail of the thread around the bundle several times and tie it off with a double knot (see diagram 2). Flatten the fabric so that it looks like a collection of petals.

3. Putting it all together

Cut – or for a nice frayed effect tear – two strips of fabric 2 cm x 30 cm. Put a dab of hot glue on the bottom end of your headband and secure the strip of fabric to it. Wrap the fabric tightly around the headband, slightly overlapping each time until you reach the other end of the headband. Secure with another dab of hot glue and trim the remainder of the fabric away.

4. Add leaves

Experiment on some paper with drawing a leaf shape and, when you are happy, transfer this design to your felt and cut out four pieces. Join two of the leaf shapes together and sew around the shape with a running stitch (see diagram 3). Repeat this with the other two felt leaf shapes.

5. Add feathers

Grab your feathers and play around with arranging the felt leaves and the feathers, then attach them with a small dab of hot glue to the side of your headband and wrap a small piece of felt around the base (see diagram 4), gluing this firmly to the headband.

6. Finishing

Put a small dab of hot glue in the centre of the flower and place the button on top, pressing down firmly (see diagram 5). Put a dab of hot glue on the felt at the base of the leaves and feathers and press your flower down firmly to the surface (see diagram 6).

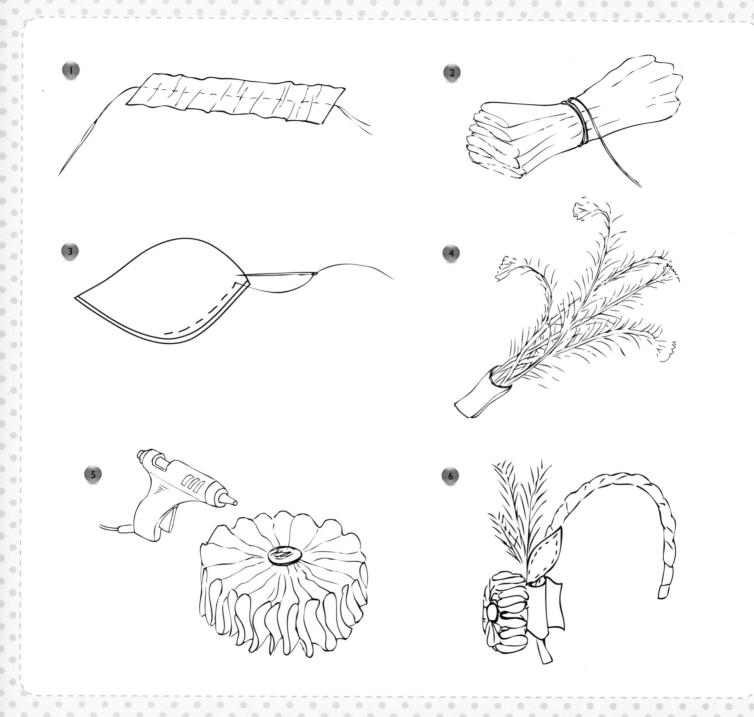

Plush Pin

These little raindrops and clouds can make any day a sunny day! Each cloud or raindrop can be made into a pendant for a necklace, a brooch, or a charm to clip on a backpack or bag. Add beads or make a series of raindrops with different expressions for a mobile. You will learn a couple of basic hand stitches for this project and there is room for more hand stitching if you like.

project by: cassi griffin
suitable for: beginners
should take: 1–2 hours

SHOPPING LIST

- Small scraps of wool or craft felt
- Black and white embroidery thread
- Toy stuffing
- Crochet or knitting yarn, string, hemp, leather or chain for your necklace; make sure the thread is cut long enough to go over your head after it has been knotted.
- Brooch pin back, large safety pin or charm clip
- Colourful seed beads (with a large enough hole to slide onto your safety pin)

CRAFTY NEEDS

- Scissors
- Embroidery needle

TEMPLATES

You will need the 'Plush pin' templates for this project.

GET READY

- Gather your tools and materials and clear some space on a sturdy work table. Make sure you have a comfy chair and some good lighting.
- Trace or photocopy the templates required onto paper and cut them out and label them, then store them in a marked envelope so that you can use them again and so they don't get wrecked.
- Take care when using sharp needles or scissors. Read the section on page 19 about safe handling of these items and be sure to put everything away carefully when you are done.
- You'll be doing some hand-sewing, but don't worry if you have never sewn before. Your stitches don't have to be perfect, and you will find some sewing basics on page 17, but you will need a basic sewing kit (page 11) to get started.
- For this project you will be using either wool felt or craft felt sheets, which you can find in most craft or sewing shops. You will also need some beads and brooch backs: you can also get these in a craft shop, or substitute a large safety pin for the brooch back.

HOW TO MAKE

1. Make the charm
Using the templates, cut two raindrops (or two clouds) from your felt. Then use three strands of black embroidery thread or floss and embroider a face onto one of the raindrop pieces; use three straight stitches for the eyes and a backstitch for the mouth (see diagram 1).

2. Make a pendant
If you are making a pendant, use the pattern to cut out a small rectangle from felt and sew it onto the back of the other raindrop (see diagram 2). Use a neat stitch and sew only across the top and bottom of the rectangle.

3. Match up the front and back raindrop pieces
Place the matching pieces together, with the right sides facing outwards, and stitch together with three strands of white embroidery thread or floss and a running stitch close to the edge (see diagram 3). Leave a 3 cm opening at the bottom, stuff lightly with toy stuffing, then stitch the opening closed.

4. If you are making a brooch
Stitch a pin or brooch back onto the back of the raindrop using three strands of white floss (see diagram 4).

5. If you are making a pendant

Cut a piece of yarn or other string that is long enough to fit over your head after it is tied in a knot. Pull the yarn through the felt loop you sewed on earlier (see diagram 2) and then tie the ends in a knot to complete your necklace.

6. If you are making a bag charm

Slide a large safety pin through the seams at the top of the raindrop. Add beads onto the safety pin if you like (see diagram 5).

7. Add beads to the shapes

Make a knot at the end of three strands of embroidery floss – make the knot large enough so the beads cannot fall off. Thread five beads onto the floss.

With the beads threaded on, pull the thread up through the bottom centre of the raindrop between the seams. Knot at the top of the raindrop. Repeat to make three more strands and place them either side of the previous strand (see diagram 5).

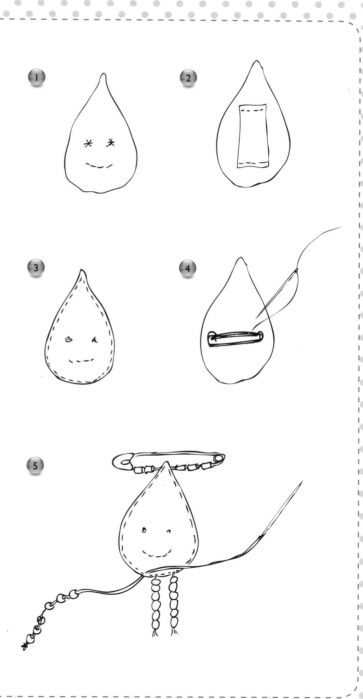

Cuff Watch

Is it a watch, is it a wrist warmer, a sweatband or wearable art? These felt cuffs have watch face designs but you could mix it up with any sort of design you like. A combination of wet felting and simple embroidery, plus a single metal press-stud closure, make these accessories simple and addictive to make.

project by: suzie fry
suitable for: beginners
should take: 2–3 hours

SHOPPING LIST

- Plain wool felt for the watch face
- Wool roving for wet felting
- Embroidery thread or floss
- A medium-sized press stud (either the hammer-in or sew-in type)
- Warm soapy water (detergent is fine)

CRAFTY NEEDS

- Scissors
- Ruler
- Bubble wrap
- Elastic bands
- An old towel
- Embroidery needle
- A small hammer (if using a hammer-in press stud)

GET READY

- Gather your tools and materials and clear some space on a sturdy work table. Make sure you have a comfy chair and some good lighting.
- Take care when using sharp needles or scissors. Read the section on page 19 about safety and put everything away carefully when you are done.
- You'll be doing some hand sewing, but don't worry if you have never sewn before. Your stitches don't have to be perfect, and you will find some sewing basics on page 17, but you will need a basic sewing kit (page 11) to get started.
- For this project you will be wet felting: it can get a bit messy, so you might want to do this project in the kitchen or outside. Read up on page 15 for more detailed information about wet felting. A press-stud closure is used here, but you could also use the loop and button closure from the 'Cup cosy' instructions (on page 64) instead.

HOW TO MAKE

1. Preparation
Cover your work table with an old towel to soak up any water that you will spill. Lay out a piece of bubble wrap on top of the towel. Have your wool roving ready nearby but out of the way of the water, and have a bowl of warm sudsy water ready.

2. Laying out the fibres
Take a small piece of roving and pull it to get long thin threads of fibre. Lay out a single, even layer of long fibres running from end to end onto your bubble wrap into a rough rectangle shape about 25 cm long and 8 cm wide (see diagram 1).
Add a second layer of fibres running across the first layer in the other direction. Add another long layer the same as the first and then add a few contrasting decorative pieces of fibre on top.

3. Get wet!
Start by wetting the laid-out fibres with hot soapy water. Sprinkle water over the roving and gently pat it down, being careful not to move any of the fibres around just yet. This first part requires gentle handing so your design does not get messed up. Continue to sprinkle and pat until it is all thoroughly wet. Then lay another piece of bubble wrap on top, carefully roll it up tightly (see diagram 2) and secure the ends with elastic bands (see diagram 3).

4. Rock and roll
Roll the sausage of bubble wrap backwards and forwards. Press down hard and move your hands around to get an even amount of pressure along the length of the sausage. Roll back and forth about 10 times and then take the elastic bands off and unroll the felt. Smooth the piece out and pull it into shape if it is getting a bit wonky.

5. Beat it
Next turn the felt sideways, roll it back up in the bubble wrap and repeat the rolling process. You can get rough with it now: you need to roll, turn, roll and turn several times until your felt is thick and strong enough to make your cuff. It will shrink quite a bit, so check it on your wrist as you go so it doesn't shrink too much. When you are happy with the size and thickness of your felt, rinse it in cold water, squeeze out the extra water and leave to dry.

6. Finishing
Make the watch face. Using light-coloured wool felt, cut a circle (or square) of felt almost as wide as the width of your cuff. Carefully embroider numbers on the watch face using embroidery thread or floss and simple straight lines – just like the numbers on a digital clock. Then add some watch hands, too. Finally, use a small running stitch to sew the watch face to the cuff (see diagram 4).

7. Add a press stud

Hammer on your press stud following the instructions on the packet (see diagram 5), or you could use the sew-on kind. Put the top half of the snap on one side of your cuff and then try it on your wrist to work out where to place the other half.

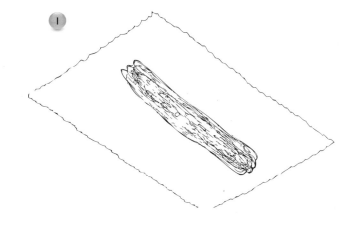

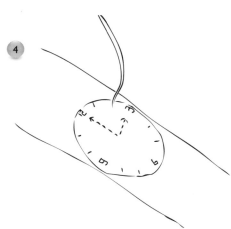

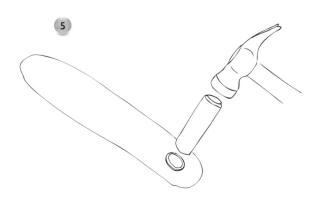

jazz your stuff

Accessorising doesn't have to mean jewellery – *you can add a bit of jazz to your stuff in other ways too. Make a cover for your journal, a charm to hang from your bag or a cosy cover for your favourite cup. Making these little treasures is a great way to learn new skills and be an individual – and the projects in this section make awesome gifts too!*

These projects are all pretty simple, but some might need a bit more time and patience than others. You will be learning some basic sewing techniques, and playing with bright fun colourful felt to create your designs. The designs shown here can be mixed and matched: try the 'Cup cosy' design on your wallet, or you could enlarge the iPod case to make a bag – just add a strap! There are so many possibilities, and no reason not to get making straight away. So grab a snack plate and your iPod, gather your materials and get cracking!

eraser heads

book blanket

ipod animals

cute cup cosy

zombie critter charms

designer wallet

Eraser Heads

These fuzzy pencil toppers will hang out on top of your pencil and make you smile as you draw or do your homework. A simple process of cutting and wrapping makes them a snap to make. Create happy, sad, angry or manic eraser heads to suit your every mood just by changing their facial expressions.

project by: ellen luckett baker
suitable for: beginners
should take: less than an hour

SHOPPING LIST

- 4 cm x 16 cm square piece of felt for each topper
- Red embroidery thread or floss
- Small buttons (about 1 cm)
- Black sewing thread

CRAFTY NEEDS

- Scissors
- Pencil
- Hand-sewing kit
- Craft glue
- Masking tape

GET READY

- Gather your tools and materials and clear some space on a sturdy work table. Make sure you have a comfy chair and some good lighting. These are so much fun and quick to make, you might want to invite some friends around for a crafty crafternoon.
- Take care when using sharp needles or scissors. Read the section on page 19 about safe handling of these items and be sure to put everything away carefully when you are done.
- This project requires some hand sewing, but don't worry if you have never sewn before. Your stitches don't have to be perfect, and you will find some sewing basics on page 17, but you will need a basic sewing kit (page 11) to get started.
- For this project you will need some basic craft felt sheets and some small colourful buttons that you can find in any craft or sewing shop.

Meet me at
the corner shop
at 4pm
X H

HOW TO MAKE

1. Cut your felt

You will need a 4 cm × 16 cm rectangle for one topper. Cut 5 cm deep slits every 1.5 cm along the long side (see diagram 1).

2. Create the face

Roll the felt onto your pencil top to see where the face should go. Hold the felt completely wrapped around the pencil top and draw the face on the front with a pencil.

3. Finishing the face

Unroll the felt, stitch the button eyes in place and embroider the mouth with a small neat backstitch (see diagram 2). Add any other details you like at this point (for example, hair bows and moustaches).

4. Glue the topper in place.

Roll the felt back onto the pencil, this time placing a small piece of masking tape to secure it at the beginning. Roll carefully and make sure that it is nice and tight (see diagram 3). When you reach the end, place a line of glue along the underside of the edge of the felt and press firmly in place (see diagram 4). Use a piece of masking tape to secure the felt until it's completely dry (about an hour).

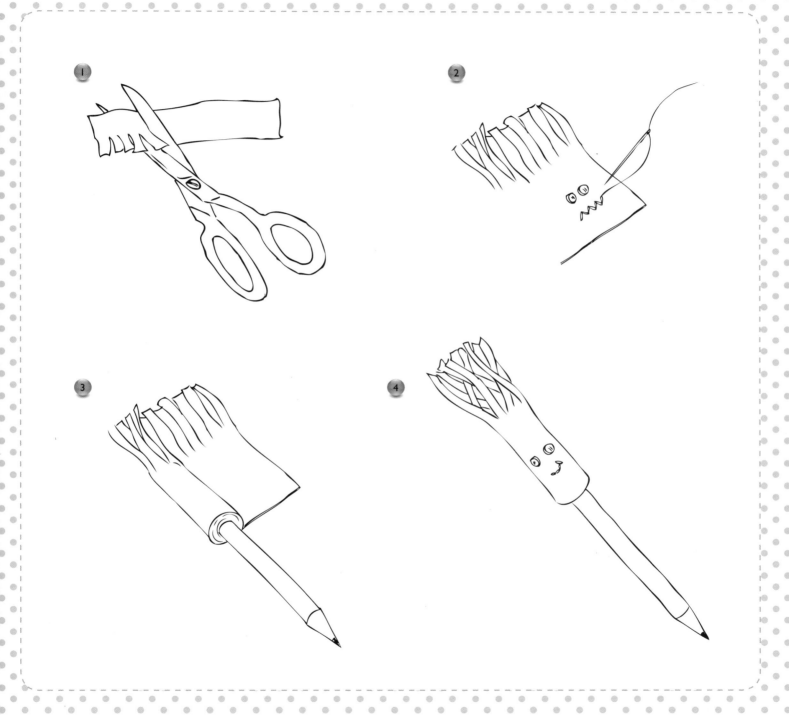

Book Blanket

With a little imagination and some colourful felt, you can create your own notebook cover perfect for outfitting your secret journal or your favourite sketchbook. If you have a sewing machine, great; but if not, this excellent book blanket is the perfect project to use your sewing-by-hand skills!

project by: christine chitnis
suitable for: beginners
should take: less than an hour

SHOPPING LIST

• Spiral-bound notebook
• 25 cm square of felt
• Small colourful scraps of felt
• Embroidery needle and thread
• Buttons, sequins and embellishments

CRAFTY NEEDS

• Measuring tape
• Pencil
• Scissors
• Pins
• Sewing machine or hand-sewing kit

TEMPLATES

You will need the 'Book blanket' templates for this project.

GET READY

• Gather your tools and materials and clear some space on a work table. Make sure you have a comfy chair and good lighting.
• Trace or photocopy the templates required onto paper and cut them out and label them, then stash them in a marked envelope so that you can use them again and so they don't get wrecked.
• Take care when using sharp needles or scissors. Read the section on page 19 about safety and be sure to put everything away carefully when you are done.
• You'll be doing some hand sewing, but don't worry if you have never sewn before. Your stitches don't have to be perfect. If you are using a sewing machine, read up on the basics on page 11 and, if you plan on hand sewing, you will need a basic sewing kit (page 11) to get started.
• For this project you will be using sheets of craft felt in different colours that you can find in most craft shops.

HOW TO MAKE

1. Measure your notebook

Measure around the spine of your notebook, starting at the inside edge of one cover and ending at the inside edge of the other cover. Then, measure the height of the notebook and add 1 cm for seam allowance. Cut a rectangle of felt to these dimensions. The felt should wrap around to the inside of both covers. This is your base felt cover. Make a slight pencil mark at the edge of the front cover and the spine (see diagram 1). This marks the point where you will place your design.

2. Create geometric designs

To make a simple geometric design, cut out two small circles, a square, a triangle and a rectangle all from different coloured felt. Arrange them as you like on the front of your felt cover, then place a dab with your glue stick on each piece to hold it in place (see diagram 2). Use your embroidery needle and thread to stitch around each shape using a simple running stitch. You could also stitch them on with your sewing machine.

3. Create flower designs

To make the flower design, cut three free-form flower shapes in different colours – you will need three large, three medium and three smaller flowers to layer on top of each other – and cut out three free-form leaf shapes in green felt. Layer your sets of flowers to create three flowers and place a dab of glue in the middle of each to hold them in place. Use a fancy button or bead to sew through the centre of the flower onto the book cover to hold them in place. Lay a leaf underneath the petals of each flower and run a line of hand stitching along each leaf in green thread to hold it in place. If you like, you can also sew on a couple of beads and buttons for extra bling (see diagram 3).

4. Handy pen holder

Add a pen holder on the edge. Cut a small rectangle (10 cm x 5 cm) from felt. Measure the halfway point between the top of your felt cover and the bottom on the outer edge. Cut a slit large enough for your small rectangle (see diagram 4). Fold the rectangle in half, insert the raw edges into the slit and sew the slit closed (see diagram 5).

5. Finishing

Once your decorations are complete and your pen holder is in place, wrap your felt once again around your book and mark the fold lines, then take the book out and pin the felt in place (see diagram 4). Machine or hand sew along the top and bottom edges to create the envelope, slip in your notebook and your project is complete!

iPod Animals

These cute iPod cases are completely hand sewn. Do you like bunnies or pigs best?
Maybe you could design your own: how about a fox, owl or monkey?
The designs here will fit most mp3 players and even your phone, but you could
customise them to be any size you need, even adding a bag strap if you like.

project by: nicole vaughan
suitable for: confident beginners
should take: 1–2 hours

SHOPPING LIST

- Good quality wool craft felt
- Embroidery thread or floss
- Buttons or sequins
- Velcro dots
- Glue stick

CRAFTY NEEDS

- Scissors
- Hand-sewing kit
- Sewing machine

TEMPLATES

You will need the 'iPod animal' templates
for this project.

GET READY

- Gather your tools and materials and clear
  some space on a sturdy work table. Make
  sure you have a comfy chair and some
  good lighting.
- Trace or photocopy the templates
  required onto paper, cut them out and
  label them. Stash them in a marked
  envelope so that you can use them again
  and so they don't get wrecked.
- Take care when using sharp needles, an
  iron or scissors. Read the section on page
  19 about safety and put everything away
  carefully when you are done.
- You'll be doing some hand sewing, but
  don't worry if you have never sewn before.
  Your stitches don't have to be perfect, and
  you will find some sewing basics on page
  17, but you will need a basic sewing kit
  (page 11) to get started.
- For this project use wool felt sheets
  available from good craft shops. You could
  also use craft felt, but get the thicker sort.

DSR
south recordings
AMI
We're Going
WARP
iPhone
16GB
CAT NO: UPFT 89
CHAPPELL MUSIC LTD
PRT

HOW TO MAKE

1. Preparation

Cut out your three pieces of felt depending on the size of the iPod you have. The two longer pieces of felt will enclose your iPod and the shortest one will be the pocket for your headphones. The longest piece of felt will be the front of your cosy.

2. Add the fasteners

Sew two Velcro dots to the underside of the front, stitching a vertical line through each dot to secure it. Repeat for the second longest piece of felt (see diagram 1).

3. Choose your design

Are you making the bunny or pig design? Cut out the extra pattern pieces you'll need, and arrange the face, arms and hands in place on your front piece. Hold the pieces in place temporarily with a dab from your glue stick.

4. Attaching the features

Start sewing the features onto your cosy with embroidery thread: in most cases you can use a simple running stitch. Use whipstitch to attach the ears.

5. Making the pouch

Once you have finished sewing the features onto the front of your cosy you can sew the pouch together. Grab all three felt pieces that you cut out in step 1, and stack them on top of each other with the bottom edges aligned and the top edges all slightly staggered – longest piece at the back and the shortest at the front. The back and middle pieces should have the Velcro attached at the top and facing forwards (see diagrams 2 and 3).

Take three strands of embroidery floss and tie a knot in one end. Thread your needle with these three strands and, holding the stack of felt pieces, insert your needle between the longest and middle piece and start a running stitch from the top of the middle piece of felt and through both layers until you come upon the third, shortest layer and start stitching through all three.

6. Adding the arms

Pin the arms onto the stack and, when you reach these, sew through all four layers, pulling nice and tight. Keep stitching around until you get to the other side and include the other arm (see diagram 4). When you get back to just sewing through the two longer pieces, tie off your thread.

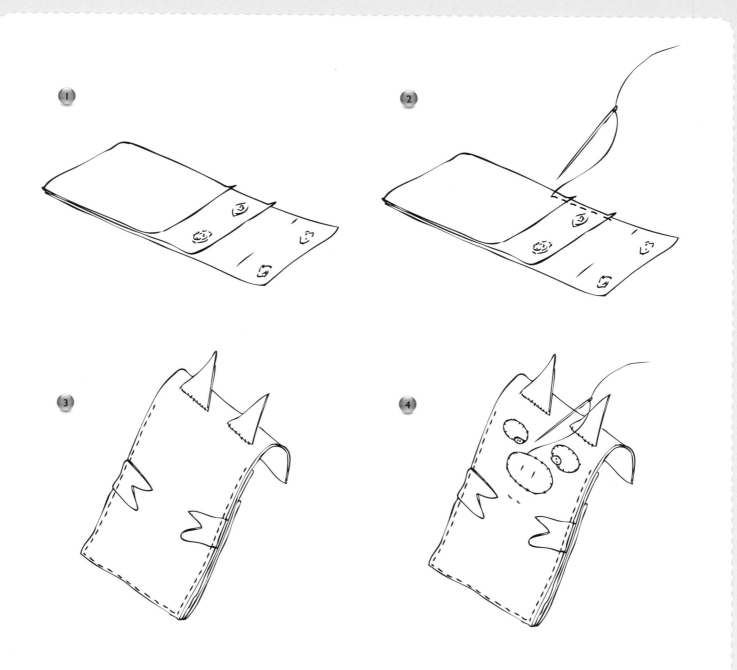

Cute'n Cup Cosy

Cuten up a cup with a fun felt cosy, to help keep cold drinks from freezing your fingers, and hot drinks from burning them. Make a quirky zombie or a happy strawberry design in fun craft felt. These cosies are completely hand sewn, but because it's such a small project it still won't take too long, and you get to practise your skills while making something totally sweet!

project by: monica solorio-snow astoria
suitable for: confident beginners
should take: 1–2 hours

SHOPPING LIST

- 30 cm square piece of felt in black for the zombie or pink for the strawberries
- Three 7.5 cm squares of felt in bright colours and in five in white
- 3–5 small buttons in bright colours
- A medium-sized button
- An elastic hair band (hair elastic)
- Embroidery thread or floss to match your felt

CRAFTY NEEDS

- Scissors
- Pencil
- Hand-sewing kit

TEMPLATES

You will need the 'Cute'n cup cosy' templates for this project.

GET READY

- Gather your tools and materials and clear some space on a sturdy work table. Make sure you have a comfy chair and some good lighting.
- Trace or photocopy the templates required onto paper, cut them out and label them. Stash them in a marked envelope so that you can use them again and so they don't get wrecked.
- Take care when using sharp needles or scissors. Read the section on page 19 about safe handling of these items and be sure to put everything away carefully when you are done.
- You'll be doing some hand sewing, but don't worry if you have never sewn before. Your stitches don't have to be perfect, and you will find some sewing basics on page 17, but you will need a basic sewing kit (page 11) to get started.
- For this project you will use good quality wool felt sheets available from good craft shops. You could also use craft felt, but get the thicker sort.

HOW TO MAKE

1. Preparation

Cut out all pieces using the templates. For the zombie cosy, cut three large circles for the zombies from different colours, cut three small circles for zombie faces from white felt, cut two base pieces from black felt. For the strawberry cosy, cut one each of the three strawberries from red felt, cut five flowers from white felt, cut three strawberry tops from green felt, cut two bases from pink or yellow felt.

2. Make the zombie cosy

Take your black felt base pieces, one for the back, and one for the decorative top. On the top piece, attach the colourful large circles using a blanket stitch in matching embroidery thread. Next attach the white circles for the faces with blanket stitch and white thread (see diagram 1).

Make the 'X' for the eye using brightly coloured thread, and stitch the mouth in dark grey thread. Sew on a button for the other eye. Make each complete zombie face so that the circle, the eye 'X' and the button are all different colours.

Embellish the top with white cross-stitch 'sparkles' and then stitch random aqua, green and purple French knots in their centres. Securely attach the medium-sized button to the centre of the top piece's long right edge.

3. Make the strawberry cosy

Take your pink felt base pieces, one for the back and one for the decorative top. On the top piece, attach the cut-out felt strawberries using blanket stitch in matching thread. Stitch six French knots with grey embroidery thread or floss to make the seeds, then sew the green leaves onto the strawberry tops with green embroidery thread or floss (see diagram 2).

Sew the white flowers with white embroidery thread or floss to the top using a simple long stitch. Stitch small yellow buttons with yellow embroidery thread or floss to the centre of the white flowers. Securely attach a medium-sized button to the centre of the top's long right edge.

4. Final assembly

For both the zombie and strawberry cosies, securely sew a hair band or hair elastic to the centre of the inside left edge to make a loop for the button (see diagram 3).

Layer the decorative top and plain bottom base pieces, making sure the decorated sides are facing outwards. Blanket stitch around the edges to complete your cup cosy.

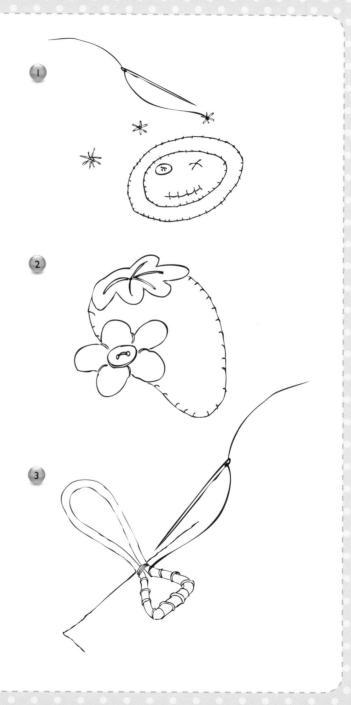

Zombie Critter Charms

Have fun making these charms – the characters you can create are limited only by your imagination. You can use these charms to hang on your bag, on a key ring, or anywhere else. Making these critters is so addictive you won't be able to stop at just one. Luckily this project is not about being super-neat – wonky stitches and mismatched button eyes look cooler!

project by: lisa tilse
suitable for: confident beginners
should take: 1–2 hours

SHOPPING LIST

• Craft felt in various colours
• Black embroidery thread or floss
• Thread to match or contrast with the felt
• 3 cm key rings (or a piece of ribbon)
• Buttons
• Toy stuffing (or cotton balls from the supermarket)

CRAFTY NEEDS

• Scissors
• Needle
• Pins

TEMPLATES

You will need the 'Zombie critter charms' templates for this project.

GET READY

• Gather your tools and materials and clear some space on a sturdy work table. Make sure you have a comfy chair and some good lighting.
• Trace or photocopy the templates required onto paper, cut them out and label them. Stash them in a marked envelope so that you can use them again and so they don't get wrecked.
• Take care when using sharp needles or scissors. Read the section on page 19 about safe handling of these items and be sure to put everything away carefully when you are done.
• You'll be doing some hand sewing, but don't worry if you have never sewn before. Your stitches don't have to be perfect, and you will find some sewing basics on page 17, but you will need a basic sewing kit (page 11) to get started.
• For this project you will use craft felt sheets and key rings, both available from craft shops.

Bike Lock

HOW TO MAKE

1. Preparation

Pin the body shape pattern to your felt and cut out two body pieces separately. Then pin your chosen critter's pattern pieces for eyes and embellishments to the felt you've chosen and cut out each piece.

2. Make the key ring loop

To make the loop that the key ring will go through, cut a piece of felt 12 mm x 40 mm. Fold the loop in half over the key ring and pin the ends of the loop to the centre top of one body piece so it's overlapping by about 5 mm. Using three strands of black embroidery thread or floss, sew the loop in place with a big 'X'. Go over each stitch a few times to make sure it's secure. This is the back of your critter. Set aside.

3. Stitching the face

Start with the eyes. Position them in place on the front body piece and sew them on with a whipstitch. It doesn't have to be too neat – the charm of these critters is that uneven and contrasting stitches add to the crazy look. You can use felt circles or buttons for the eyes, then embroider the mouth using small straight or running stitches (see diagram 1).

Sew the remaining elements, such as hair, to the body, except for arms, legs or ears. If you are making the zombie rabbit, don't add the bandages yet.

4. Assemble the critter

Lay the back body piece right side down and, if you are adding arms or ears, lay them in place so they overlap the body piece by about 5 mm (see diagrams 1 and 2). Don't worry about the legs yet or the wings for the owl. Place the front body piece on top so it aligns with the back body piece. The right side of the front body should be facing up. Pin the back and front of the body together, with one pin in each arm or ear.

5. Stitch it up

Thread a needle with your chosen colour thread (either matching or contrasting) and tie a knot in the end. Starting at the bottom left-hand corner of the body, do a double stitch and topstitch all the way around until you get to the bottom right hand corner of the body. If you still have enough thread left to sew along the bottom, do a double stitch but don't cut the thread (see diagram 3).

6. Filling

Using small pieces of toy stuffing, carefully stuff your critter. It shouldn't be too hard or full.

7. Finishing

Pin the legs in place between the two body pieces, overlapping the body by about 5 mm. Top stitch across the bottom of the critter and finish with a double stitch. Push the needle through the critter and bring it out somewhere in the middle of the body. Pull the thread tight and cut it close to the body so the end pulls inside your critter.

8. Owl wings

Pin the four owl wings in place on the body and attach with whipstitch (see diagram 4).

9. Zombie bandages

If you're making the zombie bunny, cut lengths of white felt in 6 mm strips. Long strips are better than short ones. Starting behind one ear, sew one end of the bandage in place using small stitches in off-white thread. Wrap the bandage around and around the bunny at different angles. End the bandage on the back of the bunny, so cut some off if you need to. Sew the end of the each piece of felt to the back of the bunny. Repeat with more felt bandages, covering each end with a new bandage, until your bunny is covered.

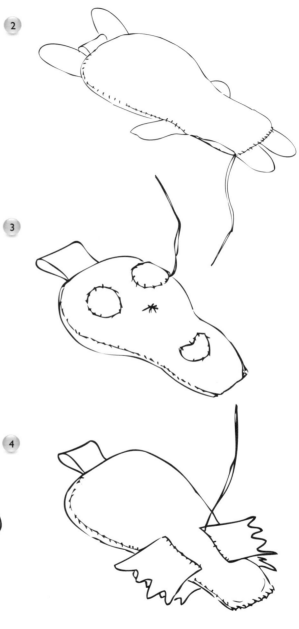

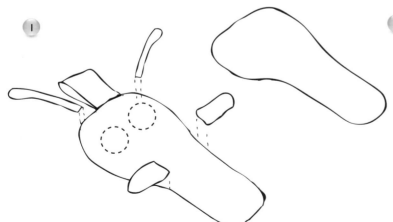

Designer Wallet

These stylish felt wallets are all you need to hold your money safely tucked away when you are out and about. The front of the wallet makes a fantastic canvas for your artistic talents: make the rocket or balloon design, or mix it up and use the designs from the 'Cup cosy', or make up your own design. These wallets are so useful and cool that all your friends will want one too.

project by: claire dollan
suitable for: confident beginners
should take: 2–3 hours

SHOPPING LIST

- Felt in assorted colours
- Embroidery thread or floss in assorted colours
- Glue stick

CRAFTY NEEDS

- Scissors
- Pencil
- Hand-sewing kit
- Sewing machine

TEMPLATES

You will need the 'Designer wallet' templates for this project.

GET READY

- Gather your tools and materials and clear some space on a work table. Make sure you have a comfy chair and good lighting.
- Trace or photocopy the templates required onto paper, cut them out and label them. Stash them in a marked envelope so that you can use them again and so they don't get wrecked.
- Take care when using sharp needles or scissors. Read the section on page 19 about safety and be sure to put everything away carefully when you are done.
- This project requires some sewing, but don't worry if you have never sewn before. Your stitches don't have to be perfect. If you are using a sewing machine read up on the basics on page 11, and if you plan on hand sewing you will need a basic sewing kit (page 11) to get started.
- For this project you will use quality wool felt sheets available from good craft shops. You could also use thick craft felt.

HOW TO MAKE

1. Preparation
Trace your designs onto paper to make your pattern pieces then cut out all the pieces from felt in the colours you want.

2. Create your design
Put a dab of glue from your glue stick on all of your design pieces and position them on the front of the wallet front (piece #2). Sew around the edges of the felt using a hand stitch – running stitch is fine, but if you like you could use blanket stitch for a stronger stitch.

3. Create your wallet pieces
Cut out another piece of felt the same size as your wallet front and place it at the back of your wallet front to cover up the back of the stitches. Use some glue to attach it in place: you will sew it on later.

4. Add Velcro pieces
Sew your Velcro to the front of your wallet, 2 cm from the right edge (see diagram 1). Sew on the soft, fuzzy (loop) piece of Velcro, centred between the top and the bottom. At the opposite end, on the reverse side, and 1 cm from edge, sew on the hard (hook) Velcro piece, centred between the top and the bottom.

5. Coin pocket
Cut out the coin pocket piece (piece #4) and sew a Velcro hook piece 1 cm from the edge, evenly spaced between the top and bottom. Line up the right side of piece #4 with the right side of piece #2, face down, and mark where the Velcro is – place the loop piece of Velcro on piece #2 to line up with the Velcro on piece #4, and sew it in place (see diagram 2).

6. Card pockets
Make a mark 2 cm in from the left-hand side of piece #2. Place back the edge of the card pockets (piece #3) at this mark, and stitch it in place with your sewing machine, close to the edge. Line up the second pocket, flush with the left edge of piece #2, and also stitch this pocket in place with your sewing machine. Reinforce along the right edge of the coin pocket, and at the top and bottom of piece #2 with a line of machine stitching, to hold the pockets in place (see diagram 3). Try to stitch as close to the edge as possible.

7. Put all the pieces together
Hand stitch the inside pocket pieces and the front piece that you decorated together. Line them up and place piece #1 face down and piece #2 facing up, with the left sides flush. Hold in place with pins or with temporary hand stitches (basting stitches), and then blanket stitch (or running stitch) your way around the outer edge, leaving the top and side edges open (see diagram 4).

8. Finishing

If you like you can add some more decorative stitching along the two top edges (but don't stitch them together), as well as the right coin purse edge so the finished wallet will have decorative stitching around all edges.

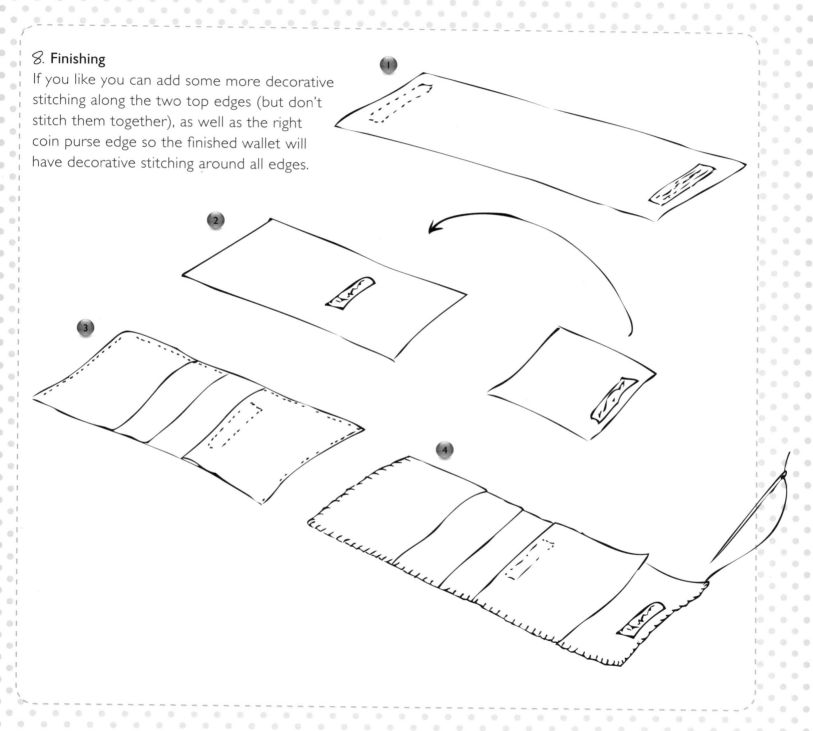

spruce your space

Whether it's your bedroom *or your favourite reading corner, getting comfortable in your space is important. Make a cosy blanket from recycled jumpers, or some cute and cuddly pet rocks with personality. These comfort items will help turn your space into a cosy corner where you can curl up with a book or your music or just hang out with friends.*

In this section you will be recycling old clothing, making felt balls and learning some basic sewing skills. There is a lot of room for individuality in these projects: change up the colours to make a blanket to suit your style or make some mini baskets that will hold your knick-knacks. So much to do, so little time — you'd better get started! Grab a fresh cookie and cup of tea, play your favourite tunes, gather some colourful felt and get making!

Zakka Stash Box

Zakka is a Japanese word to explain something that is useful, cute and simple – just like these handy boxes. These zakka boxes are easy to make and fun to use and they make cool presents too. They can be made in any size you need to stash your stuff: stationery, hair ties, favourite toys or your collections.

project by: suzie fry
suitable for: beginners
should take: less than an hour

SHOPPING LIST

- Wool felt
- Small cardboard box (such as a small tissue or tea box)
- Cotton thread or tapestry wool for sewing

CRAFTY NEEDS

- Ruler
- Scissors
- Pins
- Hand-sewing kit or sewing machine
- Pencil

GET READY

- Gather your tools and materials and clear some space on a sturdy work table. Make sure you have a comfy chair and some good lighting.
- Take care when using sharp needles or scissors. Read the section on page 19 about safe handling of these items and be sure to put everything away carefully when you are done.
- This project requires some sewing, but don't worry if you have never sewn before. Your stitches don't have to be perfect. If you are using a sewing machine read up on the basics on page 11 or, if you plan on hand sewing, you will need a basic sewing kit (page 11) to get started.
- For this project you will use good quality wool felt sheets available from good craft shops. You could also use the thicker sort of craft felt, handmade wet-felted sheets or even felted woollen jumpers.
- The size of the box you want to make will determine how much felt you will need. For the tall box you will need a 27 cm x 31 cm rectangle; for the tray you will need a 22 cm square piece of felt.

HOW TO MAKE

1. Preparation

To make the tall box, take your cardboard box and measure the base accurately. Then cut out your felt using this formula as a guideline: 2 × the height plus the base measurement in each direction. For a 7 cm × 11 cm base (and 10 cm high) box you will need a rectangle of felt that measures 27 cm × 31 cm. If you're making the tray then use your 22 cm square piece of felt (or in fact any size will work).

Cut your felt to size. Make sure your angles are properly square. Use a ruler to check.

2. Mark and sew the seams

Mark your corner seams. Fold your felt in half on the diagonal – if you have a rectangle there will be a section left over along one side. Use your ruler and pencil to mark where your side seam will be and pin it closed (see diagrams 1 and 2).

3. Stitch the seams

The seam needs to be at right angles from the top edge and will be as long as your box height. Repeat this for each corner seam. Sew the corner seams. You can use the sewing machine (with a long stitch length) or you can sew this by hand using a running stitch (see diagram 3). If your felt is thicker, hand sewing might be easier. When the seams are sewn, you can leave the extra little pieces of felt in place or you can trim them off, leaving a seam allowance of 5 mm on the outside of the box (see diagram 4).

4. Decorate your box

Use a simple running stitch design parallel to the top of the box or try embroidering your name. You could even jazz the box up with some of the embellishment ideas from the other projects in this book.

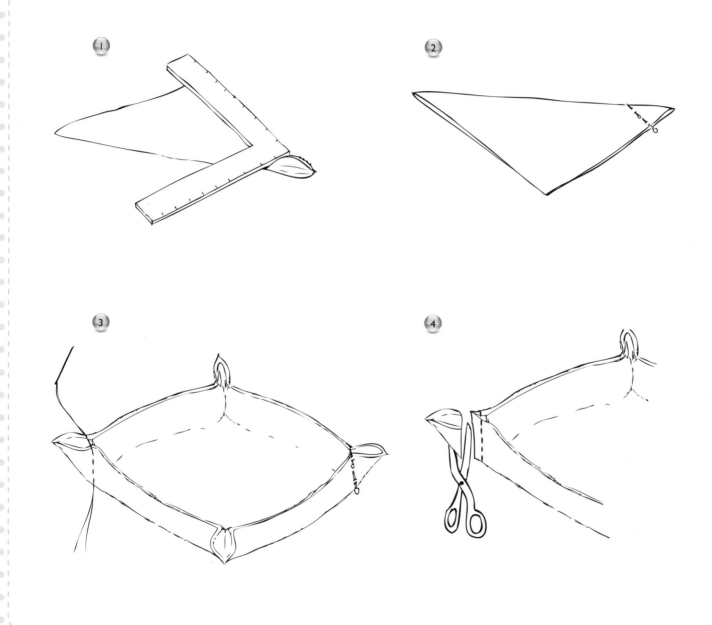

Pet Rock Stars

These zany pet rocks are ready to rock and roll! Make Mr Moustache, who is very particular, or Cutie Patutie with her long eyelashes and sweet bow tie, or how about a zombie, pirate or crazy rock. They are all made with grey felt so that they have a stone-like appearance, with a few other bits to decorate.

project by: lisa ramsey whitesell
suitable for: confident beginners
should take: 1–2 hours

SHOPPING LIST

- Black, white and grey felt
- Black, white and grey embroidery thread or floss
- Small scraps of red and blue felt
- Toy stuffing

CRAFTY NEEDS

- Hand-sewing kit
- Pins
- Scissors

TEMPLATES

You will need the 'Pet Rock' templates for this project.

GET READY

- Gather your tools and materials and clear some space on a sturdy work table. Make sure you have a comfy chair and some good lighting.
- Trace or photocopy the templates required onto paper, cut them out and label them. Stash them in a marked envelope so that you can use them again and so they don't get wrecked.
- Take care when using sharp needles or scissors. Read the section on page 19 about safe handling of these items and be sure to put everything away carefully when you are done.
- This project requires some sewing, but don't worry if you have never sewn before. Your stitches don't have to be perfect. If you are using a sewing machine read up on the basics on page 11 or, if you plan on hand sewing, you will need a basic sewing kit (page 11) to get started.
- For this project you will use wool felt sheets available from good craft shops. You could also use the thicker sort of craft felt or even felted woollen jumpers.

HOW TO MAKE

1 Make your rocks

Cut out pieces using provided templates (see diagram 1). Then use your sewing machine (set on a simple straight stitch) to sew the rock together, leaving a 10 cm gap for stuffing (see diagram 2).

2. Filling the rocks

Turn the rocks right side out and stuff with filling. Whipstitch the gap closed (see diagram 3). Make five rocks, if you are going to make all the characters here.

3. Add facial features

Temporarily position the eyes, moustache and other facial features with pins to plan how the rock will look. Thread an embroidery needle, tie a knot in the end of the thread and begin sewing behind the eye circle so that the knot is hidden. Whipstitch the eye to the rock around the entire circle. Position the other eye and bring the needle over and up through it, then whipstitch around this second eye (see diagram 4). On the final whipstitch, knot the stitch and bring the thread through the back of the rock by pulling the needle through. Snip off the thread.

Do the same with the other facial features, the eye pupil, the moustache, the eye mask and so on. If you want to add a tongue, backstitch the mouth and two-thirds of the way down the tongue, then whipstitch the tongue to the mouth – you can add teeth in the same way too. To add eyelashes, whipstitch the white eye to the rock, then add some straight stitches above the eye. Freckles are made with French knots and the bow tie is made from pretty ribbon hand sewn to the top of the rock.

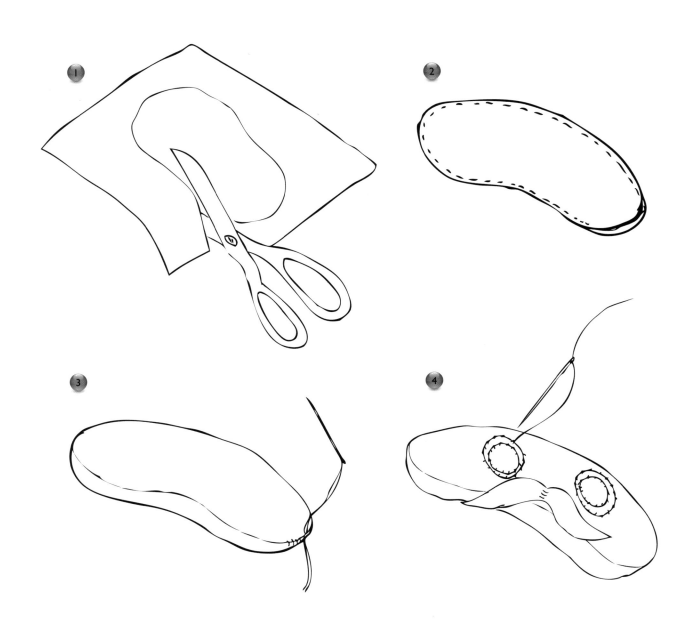

Who Loves Ewe

Make this cute trio of felt wall-hangings for your bedroom or as a gift for a special person who will appreciate your handiwork. 'Who' is Ollie the Owl hooting at his friends, Georgie the Bunny spreads the 'Love' and Gracie the sheep is a girl 'Ewe' ... Who Loves Ewe? Your little friends on the wall, of course!

project by: Cate Holst
suitable for: beginners
should take: 1–2 hours

SHOPPING LIST

- 3 stretched canvases 12.7 cm x 12.7 cm x 3.7 cm deep (from art or craft shops)
- Felt — light pink, dark pink, dark red, white, cream, tan and mid green
- Crochet, fabric or paper flowers or buttons
- Fabric glue
- Black felt-tip marker
- Little craft pompom for bunny tail
- Removable Velcro to hang frames

CRAFTY NEEDS

- Scissors
- Ruler
- Pins

TEMPLATES

You will need the 'Who loves ewe' templates for this project.

GET READY

- Gather your tools and materials and clear some space on a sturdy work table. Make sure you have a comfy chair and some good lighting.
- Trace or photocopy the templates required onto paper, cut them out and label them. Stash them in a marked envelope so that you can use them again and so they don't get wrecked.
- Take care when using sharp needles or scissors. Read the section on page 19 about safe handling of these items and be sure to put everything away carefully when you are done.
- For this project you will use craft felt sheets available from craft shops. Don't be afraid of using lots of bright and fun colours. Dark colours work really well on the background, and if you can't get the crochet flowers you can use decorative buttons instead.
- You can use any size and depth of pre-stretched canvas: simply enlarge or reduce the designs to fit.

HOW TO MAKE

1. Cover your canvases

For 12.7 x 12.7 x 3.7 cm canvas, cut out a 20 cm square piece of felt. For other sizes, measure the depth (x 2) and front to calculate the total amount of felt required to cover all sides.

Carefully position the canvas in the middle of the felt square and cut four slits in line with the top and bottom of the canvas edge to create the tabs (see diagram 1). Spread glue on to the front of the canvas and place it down on the centre of the felt square. Adhere the sides to the canvas by folding down the tabs first and then glue and adhere to the other sides over the tabs, applying more glue where necessary, to make a clean seam (see diagram 2).

2. Placing the animals

Trace or photocopy the animal templates and pin them to the felt, trace around them and cut out their shapes.

3. Bunny hanging

For the bunny, glue and adhere felt hearts to the bunny canvas then attach the bunny body and then the cheeks, nose and inner ears. Do not glue the legs down, as they should hang over the edge of the canvas (see diagram 3).

4. Owl and sheep hangings

For the owl and the sheep, glue on the bird body first. Don't glue the wings or legs down, as they should hang down over the canvas. Glue on the eyes and beak or nose and glue on some crochet, fabric or paper flowers (or buttons).

5. Finishing touches

Glue and adhere the underneath body sections to the canvas sides and fold back the feet. Glue the little pompom underneath the bunny. Lastly, draw on the eye details with a black felt-tip marker.

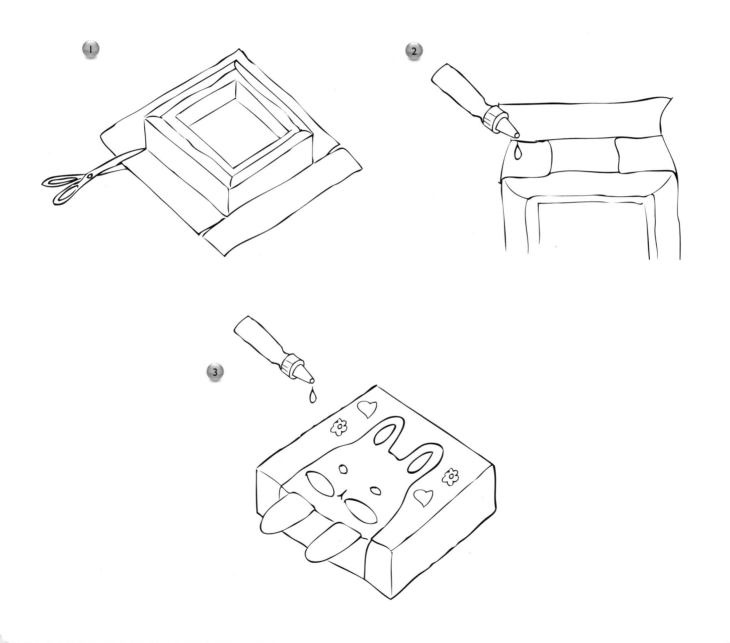

Mixed-Up Comforter

This blanket is made from recycled, felted woollen jumpers and other woollen clothing. You will need to raid the family's moth-eaten jumper pile or else head to the second-hand clothing shop. Be sure to keep in mind a colour scheme while you search for second-hand jumpers, and get ones that are not too bulky – when you felt them they will thicken up even more.

project by: kathreen ricketson
suitable for: confident beginners
should take: 2–3 hours

SHOPPING LIST

- Pieces of felt from felted woollen jumpers and other woollen clothing (approximately 9 pieces 25 cm square plus 18 pieces 15 cm × 25 cm)
- Wool yarn
- Machine sewing thread

CRAFTY NEEDS

- Sewing machine
- Pins
- Hand-sewing kit

GET READY

- Gather your tools and materials and clear some space on a sturdy work table. Make sure you have a comfy chair and some good lighting.
- Take care when using an iron, sharp needles or scissors. Read the section on page 19 about safe handling of these items and be sure to put everything away carefully when you are done.
- This project requires some sewing, but don't worry if you have never sewn before. Your stitches don't have to be perfect. If you are using a sewing machine read up on the basics on page 11 or, if you plan on hand sewing, you will need a basic sewing kit (page 11) to get started.
- For this project you will use felt that you have recycled and salvaged from woollen clothing. Read about how to felt and cut up woollen jumpers on page 14.

1. Prepare your materials

Felt your second-hand woollen jumpers and other clothing following the instructions on page 14, then use the guide on page 93 to cut up the jumper. Cut out the seams (see diagrams 1 and 2), open up the sleeves and keep any interesting details that you might like to use, such as ribbed bands and cute pockets.

2. Sort into stacks

Once you have cut up your jumper and other woollen felted clothing, sort it out into piles of big and small pieces. Use a ruler and scissors to cut the larger pieces into approximately 25 cm squares. Sew the smaller pieces into larger pieces to make up a 15 cm x 25 cm piece. You will need nine 25 cm square pieces and about 18 smaller pieces.

3. Make your blocks

Take a 25 cm piece and lay it out in front of you, onto the side add a 25 cm x 15 cm piece (see diagram 3). Pin these together, then sew using a basic straight stitch on your sewing machine. Be careful not to let the felt stretch too much as you are sewing, and then use a warm iron to press open the seams. As the seam side will be showing you need to be as neat with your sewing as possible.

You will now have a 40 cm x 25 cm rectangle. Use the remaining pieces to piece together eight more of these, always pressing the seams open as you go. When piecing them together, be free with colour and textures, making sure to mix and match to get good contrasts.

4. Joining the rectangles

Once you have all your nine rectangles (40 cm x 25 cm in size) press once again with a warm iron, lay out all the pieces somewhere flat and arrange them any way you like. Then sew them together: first create three rows of three blocks, then sew the rows together to create a rectangle shape. Press the entire piece, with the seams open, and trim any unsightly wonky seams and messy thread and press again.

5. Finishing the blanket

Use a cup or bowl to trace a curved shape on each of the corners and then use your scissors to trim (see diagram 4). To finish, take a large embroidery needle and some woollen yarn and sew a running stitch right around the edges about 3 cm in from the edge, to create a border.

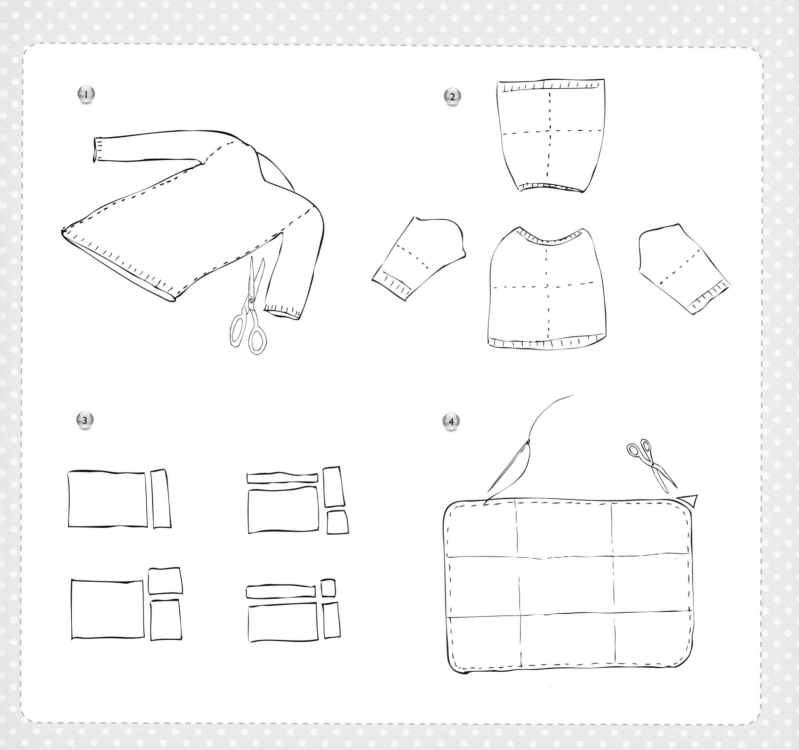

Magic Balls

Watch the magic as you transform fleecy wool into a happy ball. Not only is making these felt balls relaxing and fun, it's also a wonderful communal project, so why not get the whole family or a group of friends together for a felting crafternoon party?

project by: kathreen ricketson
suitable for: beginners
should take: 2–3 hours

SHOPPING LIST

- A mixture of different felt balls – make your own or buy ready-made felt balls from a craft store
- Crochet or embroidery thread or floss (or jewellery thread)
- Decorations: beads, wool roving, etc

CRAFTY NEEDS

- Embroidery needle
- Needle-felting needle and foam block (optional)

GET READY

- Gather your tools and materials and clear some space on a sturdy work table. Make sure you have a comfy chair and some good lighting.
- Take care when using sharp needles or scissors. Read the section on page 19 about safe handling of these items and be sure to put everything away carefully when you are done.
- For this project you can make your own felt balls from wool roving. This is fun but messy, so you will need to do this project either in the kitchen or outside. Read more about wet felting basics on page 15. To make your own felt balls you will need wool roving and a bowl of warm soapy water

HOW TO MAKE

1. Make your own felt balls

Follow the basic felt ball instructions on page 16. Make a variety of sizes, some big, some small, some wonky-shaped too if you like. While the felt is wet and before it is too compacted, you can shape it in all sorts of ways – experiment making squares or love hearts if you like.

2. Decorate

Add a bit of sparkle and decoration to your felt balls. Use a needle and thread to sew some tiny sparkly seed beads into the balls (see diagram 1). Or use the basic needle-felting instructions on page 16 to needle felt some different coloured spots of colourful roving onto your felt balls.

3. String them up

Once you have about 50 felt balls – here a mixture of bought and homemade balls have been used – thread them all onto a piece of crochet cotton, embroidery thread or floss or jewellery thread. Thread your needle with a 60 cm length, create a loop in the end and tie a knot. Thread on two or three balls at once (see diagram 2) and tie a small knot about 5 cm away from this first series of balls, then thread on a larger, more decorative, ball, tie another knot 5 cm away from this ball, and continue in this way for all of your balls (see diagram 3).

Be sure to mix up the colours, textures and sizes with your threading pattern. When you come to the end of your thread, thread some more on your needle and tie the end onto the last piece. Once you have a long enough string, tie another loop in the other end and tie it off. Hang the string of beads up somewhere that needs a bit of sparkle and colour.

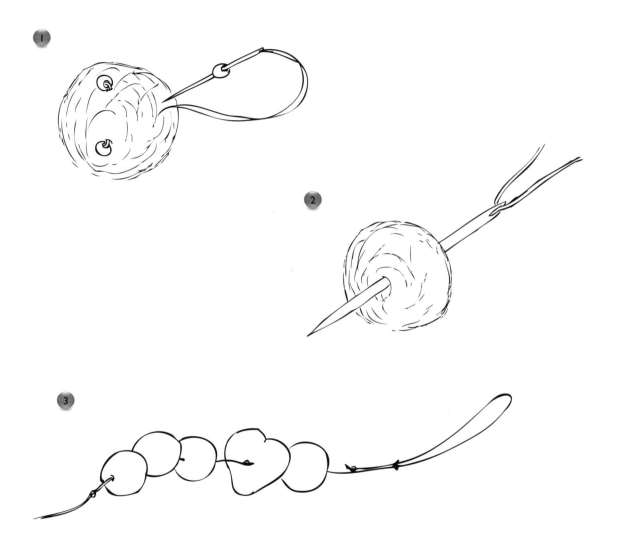

have a little fun

Who doesn't like to play and pretend and have a little fun sometimes? Here you will find a cute selection of fun playmates and activities to give your playtime a little kickstart. 'Friendly finger puppets' and a 'Beardy disguise' will give you plenty to start with, while the 'Emoticon bookmarks' will make you smile each time you open your book, and the 'Dachshund moneybox' is a fun way to hide your cash in plain view.

There is a range of projects in this chapter, a couple a bit trickier than others, but nothing super-difficult. You will be learning more advanced sewing techniques as well as mucking about with glue. Just remember to stay calm and don't fret if the result isn't perfect – it's your creative effort that counts. So grab a slice of warm cake and a glass of homemade lemonade, put some music on and make something today!

simple felt cards

emoticon bookmarks

beardy disguise

felt dartboard

friendly finger puppets

robot softie

dachshund moneybox

Simple Felt Cards

This is a great project for making any sort of card your heart could desire. The project uses felt cut into simple shapes and glued to folded sheets of cardstock to make colourful and eye-catching designs. There are so many ways to vary your designs – just use your imagination.

project by: holly keller
suitable for: beginners
should take: less than an hour

SHOPPING LIST

• A4 sheet of coloured cardstock
• Small scraps of colourful felt
• Glue stick

CRAFTY NEEDS

• Ruler and pencil
• Scissors
• Fine-tipped black marker
• Bone folder (or a butter knife)
• Awl or large needle

TEMPLATES

You will need the 'Simple felt cards' templates for this project.

GET READY

• Gather your tools and materials and clear some space on a sturdy work table. Make sure you have a comfy chair and some good lighting.
• Trace or photocopy the templates required onto paper, cut them out and label them. Stash them in a marked envelope so that you can use them again and so they don't get wrecked.
• Take your time when cutting out your pieces in felt to get the fiddly details just right.
• Take care when using sharp needles or scissors. Read the section on page 19 about safety and be sure to put everything away carefully when you are done.
• You'll be doing some hand sewing, but don't worry if you have never sewn before. Your stitches don't have to be perfect, and you will find some sewing basics on page 17, but you will need a basic sewing kit (page 11) to get started.
• For this project you will use scraps of craft felt in all sorts of colours.

HOW TO MAKE

1. Make the cards

Take a regular A4 sheet of coloured card stock and cut it in half at the midpoint on the long edge of the paper. Use a bone folder (or a butter knife) and a ruler to mark the centre of the card, then fold each piece of card stock in half on your crease mark.

2. Cut out the felt shapes

Copy and cut out your template pieces from felt (see diagram 1). Use contrasting coloured pieces of felt for the different parts of your design.

3. Assemble the design

Use your glue stick to rub glue all over the back of your felt pieces. Place them onto your card and press into place, smoothing out the felt (see diagram 2). Repeat for the rest of your designs, making sure – if you have a layered design – they are placed in the right order.

4. Write the message

Use a pencil to write your message on the card and draw any lines or designs you like. Then trace over your pencil marks with a black felt-tip marker.

5. Extras

If you like to sew, try sewing your message onto the front of your card. First write your message lightly in pencil, then punch holes into your card with an awl or large needle along the lines of your letters about every 5 mm (see diagram 3). Stitch through the holes with a contrasting coloured embroidery floss, using a simple running stitch or backstitch (see diagram 4).

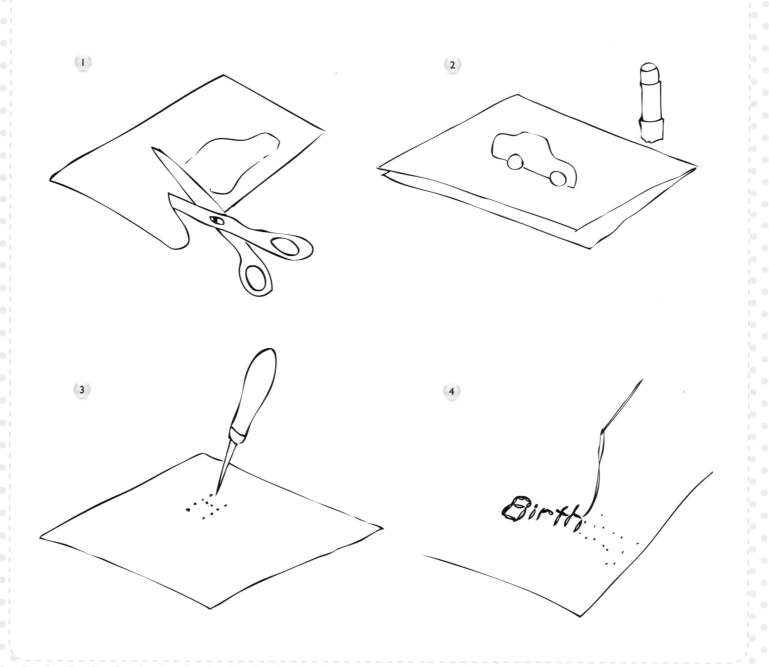

Emoticon Bookmarks

These bookmarks are embroidered with emoticon faces on felt circles. Emoticons are small picture or text-based symbols that show your feelings. For example, :-) and :-(are happy and sad faces, while :O and :D mean surprised and excited. More complex ones include (-_-) (x_x) (T_T) (ˉ.ˉ) (^_~). Can you guess what these might mean?

project by: lisa tilse
suitable for: beginners
should take: less than an hour

SHOPPING LIST

- Yellow felt
- Black embroidery thread or floss
- 12 mm wide sturdy cotton ribbon – about 30 cm for each bookmark

CRAFTY NEEDS

- Fine black felt-tip marker
- Paper and scissors
- Needle
- Hot glue gun or fabric glue

TEMPLATES

- Draw, trace, photocopy or print from the computer your own emoticons onto a piece of paper, big enough for the face.

- Draw a 4.5 cm diameter circle onto a piece of paper and cut it out.

GET READY

- Gather your tools and materials and clear some space on a sturdy work table. Make sure you have a comfy chair and some good lighting.
- Take care when using sharp needles, scissors and a hot glue gun. Read the section on page 19 about safe handling of these items and be sure to put everything away carefully when you are done.
- You'll be doing some hand sewing, but don't worry if you have never sewn before. Your stitches don't have to be perfect, and you will find some sewing basics on page 17, but you will need a basic sewing kit (page 11) to get started.
- When embroidering around curves try to keep your stitches small to achieve a smooth curve.

HOW TO MAKE

1. Preparation

Using your circle templates cut two circles of yellow felt for each bookmark. Plug in the hot glue gun so it warms up.

2. Transferring the designs

With a small piece of adhesive tape, attach the paper with the emoticons on it to a window. A window – in the daytime – is the perfect lightbox. Position a felt circle over it so that the emoticon is in the centre of the circle. Using the felt tip marker put a dot on the end points of each straight line, and on a few points of each curved line as guides for embroidery.

3. Embroider your design

Tie a knot in your thread and bring the needle up from the wrong side of the felt into one of the dot guides. Following the dot guides, and referring to the original emoticon, embroider the design. For short, straight lines use one long stitch, but for longer lines and curves use small, neat backstitches (see diagram 1). Finish with a small double stitch. Cut the ends of the thread off close to the felt on the back.

4. Attach the ribbon

Cut the ribbon so one end is straight across and the other is diagonal. Place the plain felt circle on your work surface and put a 1 cm line of hot glue across the bottom, a couple of millimetres in from the edge (see diagram 2). Place the straight edge of the ribbon on top of the glue so that it overlaps the bottom of the circle by about 5 mm. Press in place with your finger, being careful not to touch the glue while it is still hot.

5. Finishing

Draw a ring of hot glue around the circle, a few millimetres in from the edge. Position your embroidered circle on top so the edges of the circles match up and the ribbon is coming out of the bottom of the emoticon face. To finish, press the circles together with your fingers and you're done! (See diagram 3 for some ideas for faces.)

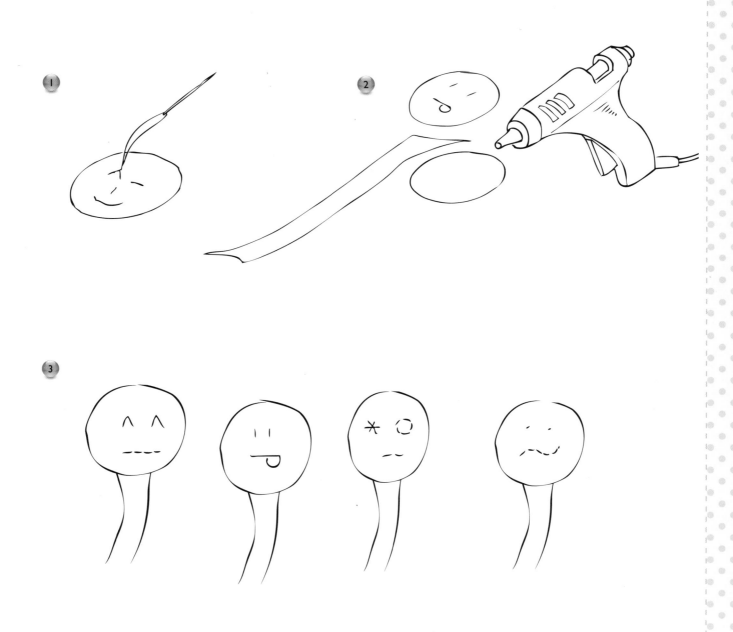

Beardy Disguise

Need a quick disguise? A fake beard or moustache will do the trick! Fool your friends and family with this fun costume. It's made entirely with craft felt and some simple stitching. You might like to make yours out of crazy colours: how does a blue beard grab you? Or you could make some crazy shaped moustaches in any design you like!

project by: erin dollar
suitable for: confident beginners
should take: 1–2 hours

SHOPPING LIST

- Two 20 cm x 30 cm pieces craft felt, in any colour
- Thread in matching colour
- 60 cm of clear elastic cord
- 1 metre of cotton ribbon, cut in half

CRAFTY NEEDS

- Hand-sewing kit or sewing machine
- Pins
- Scissors

TEMPLATES

You will need the 'Beardy disguise' templates for this project.

GET READY

- Gather your tools and materials and clear some space on a work table. Make sure you have a comfy chair and good lighting.
- Trace or photocopy the templates onto paper, cut them out and label them. Stash them in an envelope so that you can use them again and so they don't get wrecked.
- Take care when using sharp needles or scissors. Read the section on page 19 about safety and be sure to put everything back carefully when you are done.
- This project requires some sewing, but don't worry if you have never sewn before. Your stitches don't have to be perfect. If you are using a sewing machine read up on the basics on page 11 or, if you plan on hand sewing, you will need a basic sewing kit (page 11) to get started.
- For this project you need craft felt in basic colours; however, you can use any coloured felt, you will also need clear elastic cord, which you can find in craft stores.

HOW TO MAKE

1. Cutting out the beard

Trace and cut out your pattern pieces on paper. If you want to change the shape of the template, to make a different design or to shape it to fit your face better, now is the time to do so.

Stack two pieces of felt on top of each other, pin the template to the top and trace around it, then cut out the felt pieces. Remove the template and pin the pairs of felt pieces together.

2. Stitching the beard

Sew the ribbon ties to the upper right and left corners of the felt beard panel (where they will go over your ears and behind your head), sandwiching the ribbon between the felt layers to hide the end of it, then either hand or machine sew an X to hold it in place (see diagram 1).

Hand or machine sew, using a straight or running stitch, along the outer edge of the larger felt pieces, leaving about 5 mm gap along the outside. This secures the two large felt panels that make up the bottom of the beard.

3. Add the moustache

Pin the moustache pieces over the tabs on the beard, making sure to sandwich the tabs on the top of the beard inside each side of the moustache. Try to keep the moustache centred between the two top flaps (see diagram 2). With the moustache pinned in place, sew along the edge of the moustache, taking care to sew securely through all layers where the two panels meet along the tabs. If you are doing this on the sewing machine set the speed to slow so you can be extra careful. Check for stray threads, trim messy edges, and your beard is all finished!

4. Cutting out moustaches

Take your moustache templates and hold the template up to your face to imagine how the finished moustache will look. If you want to change the shape of the template, now is the time to do so. Cut out your felt as in step 1.

5. Add elastic

Measure your elastic around the circumference of your head, starting at the centre of your mouth, circling back over the ears and behind the head where the strap will rest. Cut your elastic to this length (approximately 50 cm) and tie a large knot as close to each end as possible. This will keep the elastic from slipping off.

6. Finishing

Sew along the outer edge of the felt pieces, sandwiching the knotted ends of the clear elastic between the felt layers so the end of the elastic is hidden between the two layers of felt (see diagrams 3 and 4). Sew a few reinforcing stitches to keep this in place. Be sure that the elastic is placed symmetrically on each side of the moustache, so it will lay flat on your face. Trim stray threads and messy edges. Try on your masterpiece! Add eye patches, gnome hats, or villainous-looking tattoos as needed to complete your look.

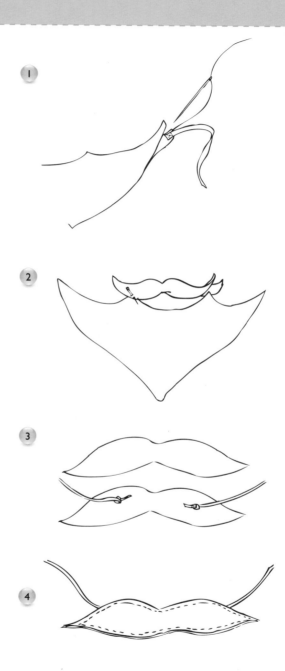

Felt Dartboard

How exciting to make your own dartboard! But remember that darts require some precautions: make sure you have a good space to set up your board and that other players are well back. Also, you might need to hang some foam board on the wall behind your dartboard to protect it from missed shots. Set up a scoreboard so you can have a real competition with friends.

project by: rob shugg
suitable for: beginners
should take: 1–2 hours

SHOPPING LIST

- 38 cm squares of black and red felt
- 17 cm square of green felt
- PVA craft glue
- Large paintbrush
- 38 cm square of cardboard from a sturdy cardboard box
- Bamboo sticks
- Small scraps of wool roving
- 30 cm of fine craft wire (24–26 gauge)
- Small sewing pins
- Cotton sewing thread
- Small scraps of coloured card stock

CRAFTY NEEDS

- Scissors
- Paintbrush
- Craft knife
- Hammer
- Wire cutters

GET READY

- Gather your tools and materials and clear some space on a sturdy work table. Make sure you have a comfy chair and some good lighting.
- Take care when using a craft knife and scissors. Read the section on page 19 about safe handling of these items and be sure to put everything back carefully when you are done. Some parts of making this project require some parental supervision.
- For this project, you can use felt from recycled jumpers. But you could use any felt including craft felt or even commercial felt, as long as it is a large enough piece.
- We've used traditional dartboard colours but you could make the board in any colours you like.

HOW TO MAKE

1. Make the dartboard base

Take a large section of cardboard from a sturdy cardboard box and draw a 38 cm diameter circle. Then, using sturdy craft scissors or a craft knife, cut out this cardboard circle. Use this as a template to cut out a 38 cm circle of black felt.

2. Attach the felt base

Squirt a big splodge of PVA craft glue onto your cardboard and spread it around with a large paintbrush. Carefully position your black felt circle onto the cardboard and press it down neatly all around so it is completely glued – check the edges are glued properly too – then leave it to dry for a bit while you cut your remaining pieces of felt.

3. Templates for the different colours

Grab three circular items from your kitchen cupboard, each one smaller than the other; try a pasta bowl (22 cm diameter), side plate (17 cm diameter) and small bowl (9 cm diameter).

4. Add the rings to the base

Take your red circle of felt and centre your largest (22 cm diameter) bowl or plate on top. Draw a circle on the felt and then use your scissors to carefully cut this out. Then cut 2.5 cm inside the circle to make a large ring shape (see diagram 1).

5. Attach the bullseye

Take your 17 cm diameter circular object and trace it onto your green felt to create the outer cutting line, then use the 9 cm diameter bowl to trace the inner circle. Cut it out to create a green felt ring. Lastly take a scrap of red felt and cut out a 4 cm circle for the bullseye (see diagram 1).

6. Cover the base

Take your black felt base and place the large red ring on the outer perimeter, then place the green ring and the small red circle in the middle. You should have rings of black felt showing through in between each of the coloured rings. Use generous amounts of PVA craft glue to attach each of these rings in position (see diagram 2), then leave it to dry for an hour. After an hour check that the edges are properly attached: if not, add more glue around the edges and press down firmly – place a sheet of baking paper and then a few books on top to weigh it down while it dries. Leave for a few hours or overnight to completely dry.

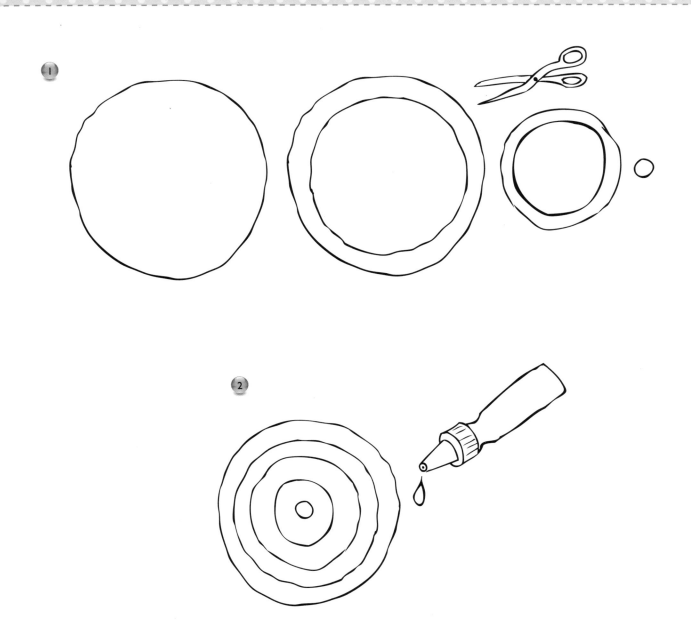

Friendly Finger Puppets

Sew a few of these basic puppet shapes and then have fun making them into all sorts of imaginative characters. Wool felt is the best material to use for this project. It comes in a variety of vibrant colours and is perfect for cutting out small features. You could make a kitty, a lion, a monkey, a pig, a lizard or any other animal you like!

project by: abby glassenberg
suitable for: confident beginners
should take: 1–2 hours

SHOPPING LIST

- Scraps of wool felt in a variety of colours
- Embroidery thread or floss in white and black
- Tiny amount of toy stuffing
- White sewing thread

CRAFTY NEEDS

- Pencil
- Scissors
- Pins
- Hand-sewing needle
- Embroidery needle
- Fabric glue

TEMPLATES

You will need the 'Friendly finger puppets' templates for this project.

GET READY

- Gather your tools and materials and clear some space on a sturdy work table. Make sure you have a comfy chair and some good lighting.
- Trace or photocopy the templates required onto paper, cut them out and label them. Stash them in a marked envelope so that you can use them again and so they don't get wrecked.
- You need to add a 5 mm seam allowance around the outside of the template when you are cutting out the shapes for this project.
- Take care when using sharp needles or scissors. Read the section on page 19 about safe handling of these items and be sure to put everything away carefully when you are done.
- This project requires some sewing, but don't worry if you have never sewn before. Your stitches don't have to be perfect. If you are using a sewing machine read up on the basics on page 11 or, if you plan on hand sewing, you will need a basic sewing kit (page 11) to get started.
- For this project you need good quality wool felt sheets or better quality craft felt available at sewing and craft shops.

HOW TO MAKE

1. Cut out the felt pieces

Use your pattern pieces to cut two body pieces and one gusset piece from one colour of felt. Remember to leave a 5 mm seam allowance around the outside edges of the templates when cutting. Transfer all markings from your pattern to the felt with your pencil.

2. Sew up the puppet

Line up point A on one body piece with point A on the gusset. Pin the gusset all the way around the body piece, ending at point B. Stitch from point A to point B. Repeat with other body piece. Then stitch from point B to point C so that the finger puppet is now completely sewn (see diagrams 1–3).

3. Trim and stuff

Trim seam allowances a little to get rid of any bulky bits, then turn the puppet right side out (see diagram 4) and stuff the head firmly with stuffing.

4. Finishing

Embellish your finger puppet with shapes cut from felt. Attach the shapes with fabric glue. Sew on a mouth with black embroidery thread or floss and sew on some eyes with white embroidery thread or floss.

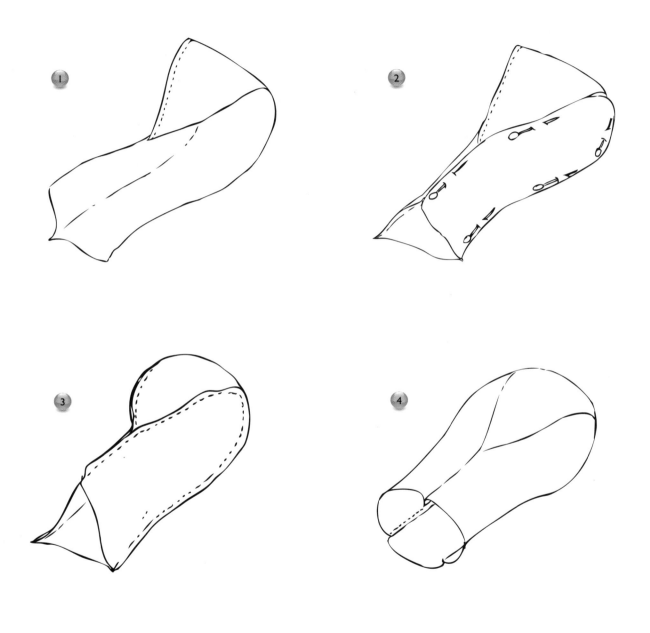

Robot Softie

This bendy robotic soft toy is über cool and is equally great to snuggle up with as to sit on your bookshelf guarding your treasures. He is really easy to customise – once you have made the basic pattern, have a go at mixing him up, you might like to turn him into an alien or monster by adding extra arms, eyes or different messages on his front panel.

project by: bianca brownlow
suitable for: beginners
should take: 2–3 hours

SHOPPING LIST

- Piece of craft felt in any colour
- Felt scraps for face, buttons and panels
- Four pipe cleaners
- Embroidery thread or floss
- Toy stuffing

CRAFTY NEEDS

- Craft glue
- Pencil or disappearing ink pen
- Hand-sewing kit or sewing machine
- Scissors
- Paper

TEMPLATES

You will need the 'Robot softie' templates for this project.

GET READY

- Gather your tools and materials and clear some space on a sturdy work table. Make sure you have a comfy chair and some good lighting.
- Trace or photocopy the templates required onto paper, cut them out and label them. Stash them in a marked envelope so that you can use them again and so they don't get wrecked.
- Take care when using sharp needles or scissors. Read page 19 about safe handling of these items and be sure to put everything away carefully when you are done.
- This project requires some sewing, but don't worry if you have never sewn before. Your stitches don't have to be perfect. If you are using a sewing machine read up on the basics on page 11 or, if you plan on hand sewing, you will need a basic sewing kit (page 11) to get started.
- In this project you use regular craft or wool felt sheets. You will also need bendy pipe cleaners, available at all craft shops.

HOW TO MAKE

1. Prepare your pieces
Fold your piece of felt in half and place the pattern pieces on top of the felt. Trace around the pattern and then cut out your felt pieces through the two layers of felt, which will give you two pieces of each. You will end up with two head pieces and two body pieces. Place one end of the arm and leg pattern on a fold in the felt. Carefully cut around the pattern and through two layers of felt. Repeat. You will have two folded legs and two folded arms. Unfold the remaining bit of felt and cut your front panel cover.

2. Making the circuit board
From a contrasting coloured scrap of felt, cut the circuit board panel. Use the pencil to write your chosen word on the panel. Use a running stitch and a few strands of embroidery thread or floss (so that the stitches come out thick) to sew along the lines of the letters and around the edge of the panel (see diagram 1).

3. Attach the circuit board
Pin the circuit board panel to the middle of one of the body pieces. Sew it on, following the line of running stitches.

4. Decorating the circuit board
Use your embroidery floss and needle to stitch around the second front panel cover (use a whipstitch or running stitch). Cut small shapes from the scrap felt to use as buttons on the panel and eyes on the face. Attach the shapes with a simple cross stitch. Position the cover panel over the circuit board panel and use a running stitch down only the left side to secure it to the body.

5. Stitch the legs
Take one folded leg piece and, with wrong sides facing, sew around three sides with your sewing machine, leave one short end open. Repeat for all arm and leg pieces. You will end up with two arms and two legs.

6. Shape the legs
Fold the pipe cleaners in half and slip one into each arm and leg, pushing the folded end in first (this will make sure you don't get any sharp bits poking through your seam after you finish). Use scissors to snip the excess off, leaving about 5 mm poking out. Twist the ends of the pipe cleaners together (see diagram 2).

7. Add the antennae
Use two of the pieces of excess pipe cleaner that you just cut off, and sandwich them between the felt antennae pieces so that the pipe cleaner sticks out of one side. Sew around all sides of the antennae.

8. Stitch the body

Take one piece of the felt body and lay it wrong side up. Position the legs and arms in place, making sure the pipe cleaner end lies over the edge. Place the other body piece on top and pin them together, then sew around three edges, leaving the top edge open for stuffing. Make sure the sewing goes across the pipe cleaners and that all the limbs are attached. It can help to go back and forth several times across the pipe cleaners to make sure they are reinforced.

9. Stitch the head

Repeat with the head pieces and antennae. This time the pipe cleaner ends should not be hidden inside the robot, but sticking up from the top. Leave the bottom side open for stuffing. Place a small amount of stuffing inside the head (see diagram 3). Don't overstuff or it will be difficult to close it. Sew the opening closed. Place a small amount of stuffing into the body. Don't overstuff it.

10. Complete the body

Slip the edge of the head inside the body opening, pin them together and sew the opening closed by hand (see diagram 4). Make sure you catch the edge of the head so it stays in place. Carefully trim any stray threads and tidy up the edges of the body, head, legs and arms to make sure they're even.

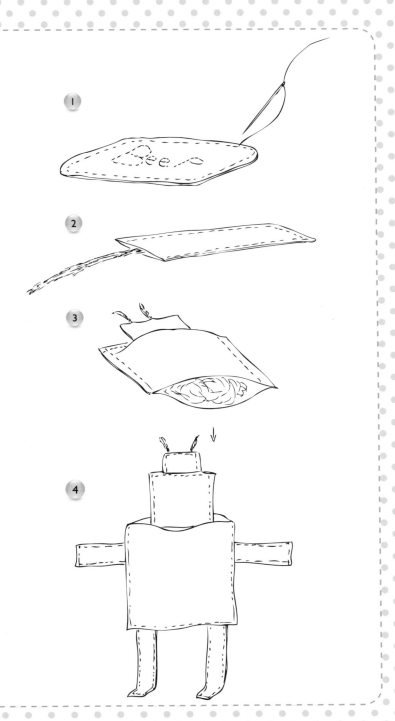

Dachshund Moneybox

This interesting sausage-dog softie has another function besides being cute.
As well as being an adorable wiener dog it is also a secret bank cleverly constructed with
a mailing tube and bits of scrap felt. Plus it's wearing a super-cute coat that nicely covers
up the money slot so you can keep this moneybox hidden in plain sight!

project by: timothy haugen
suitable for: confident beginners
should take: 2–3 hours

SHOPPING LIST

- 5 cm diameter mailing tube
- 25 cm of felt in various colours
- Some extra scraps of colourful felt
- 10 cm square piece of fun polka dot felt or fabric
- Coordinating embroidery thread or floss
- Tiny craft pompom for nose
- Toy stuffing
- Velcro
- Craft glue, such as hot glue

CRAFTY NEEDS

- Sewing machine
- Hand-sewing kit
- Scissors
- Pins
- Craft knife
- Needle with a large eye, such as a chenille needle
- Hot glue gun
- Rubber band

TEMPLATES

You will need the 'Dachshund moneybox' template for this project.

GET READY

- Gather your tools and materials and clear some space on a sturdy work table. Make sure you have a comfy chair and some good lighting.
- Trace or photocopy the templates required onto paper, cut them out and label them. Stash them in a marked envelope so that you can use them again and so they don't get wrecked.
- Take care when using a hot glue gun, iron, sharp needles or scissors. Read the section on page 19 about safe handling of these items and be sure to put everything away carefully when you are done.
- This project requires sewing by hand and by machine, but don't worry if you have never sewn before. Your stitches don't have to be perfect. Read up on the basics on page 17 or, if you plan on hand sewing, you will need a basic sewing kit (page 11) to get started.
- For this project make sure to use good quality craft felt that is available in sheets from crafting and sewing shops. You will also need a mailing tube – you can grab one from the post office or a stationery store.

HOW TO MAKE

1. Prepare your materials

Use a craft knife to cut the end of your mailing tube off so that it is 23 cm long. Mailing tubes are constructed with a heavy cardboard and may require many passes to cut all the way through. Please use caution when doing this, as craft knives are very sharp! Find the centre of the cut tube and cut a 6 mm x 4 cm slot to deposit the money.

2. Cutting out

Pin your pattern pieces to the felt and cut out the felt pieces. Cut a 23 cm x 19 cm piece of felt for the body, which will be wrapped around the mailing tube.

3. Make the body pieces

Begin sewing the head by pinning the head gusset to one of the head sides (see diagram 1). A gusset is used in sewing to make a three dimensional form. With the gusset sewn on one side, pin the other side to the gusset. Before you sew it together, fold the tongue in half and place one end into the seam of the head and pin it into place. Make sure the tongue is pointing up. Sew together to complete the head. Turn the head right side out and generously stuff the head with toy stuffing, leaving some space at the neck opening to fit the tube into.

4. Tail and ears

Fold the tail together, pin and sew the top and back. Turn right side out. Stuff the tail and sew up the opening. Pin together the pairs of ears and hand sew with blanket stitch or whipstitch around each ear. When you reach the tab on top of the ear make sure to fold it down and sew over the tab (see diagram 2). You will later sew or glue this tab to the head.

5. Sew the legs

Pin together the legs and sew a whipstitch around the leg. Before you stitch it closed, lightly stuff the leg, then finish whipstitching.

7. Assemble the dog

Put some glue around the inside edge of the neck opening on the head and glue it onto the cut end of the mailing tube. Line it up so the money slot faces upward. Secure the neck to the tube with a rubber band while the glue dries. Put glue onto the tail tab and glue it into place. When the glue has completely dried remove the rubber band.

Wrap the felt body piece around the mailing tube. Trim if necessary. Pin with the seam on the underside and sew it together with whipstitch. Cut out the felt over the money slot with a craft knife. Glue or sew the tab of the ears to the head. Glue felt eyes and the pompom nose to the head.

Glue the legs to the body with a hot glue gun. Make sure they are even and level so the puppy will stand well. Wrap the collar around her neck and sew it on with whipstitch.

Sew together the coat with the belly strap sandwiched in between the pieces (see diagram 3). Finish the coat by sewing Velcro into place where marked on the template. Wrap the coat around your dog to keep her snuggly warm and hide the money slot (see diagram 4).

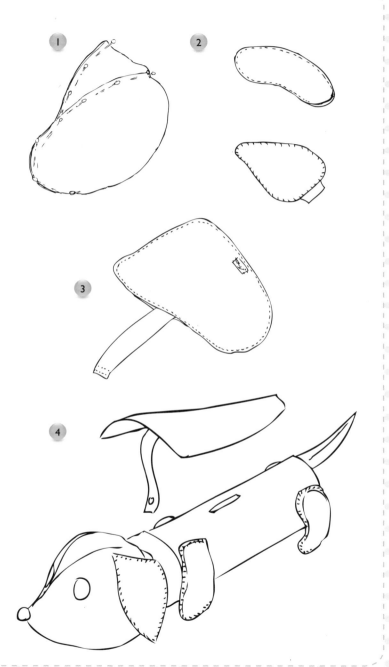

Published in 2011 by Hardie Grant Books

Hardie Grant Books (Australia)
Ground Floor, Building 1
658 Church Street
Richmond, Victoria 3121
www.hardiegrant.com.au

Hardie Grant Books (UK)
Second Floor, North Suite
Dudley House
Southampton Street
London WC2E 7HF
www.hardiegrant.co.uk

National Library of Australia Cataloguing-in-Publication Data is available
ISBN: 9781742700441 (hbk.)

Publisher: Paul McNally
Project editor: Jane Winning
Design and art direction: Heather Menzies
Photography: Alicia Taylor
Styling: Rachel Vigor
Editor: Melody Lord

Colour reproduction by Splitting Image Colour Studio
Printed in China by 1010 Printing International Limited